Introduction and Implementations of the Kalman Filter

Edited by Felix Govaers

Published in London, United Kingdom

IntechOpen

Supporting open minds since 2005

Introduction and Implementations of the Kalman Filter
http://dx.doi.org/10.5772/intechopen.75731
Edited by Felix Govaers

Contributors
Mudambi R Ananthasayanam, Xiaofeng Wu, Jeremy Soh, Lahouari Cheded, Rajamani Doraiswami, Gongjian Zhou, Youngjoo Kim, Hyochoong Bang, Felix Govaers

First published in London, United Kingdom, 2019 by IntechOpen
IntechOpen is the global imprint of INTECHOPEN LIMITED, registered in England and Wales, registration number: 11086078, The Shard, 25th floor, 32 London Bridge Street
London, SE19SG - United Kingdom
Printed in Croatia

British Library Cataloguing-in-Publication Data
A catalogue record for this book is available from the British Library

Additional hard copies can be obtained from orders@intechopen.com

Introduction and Implementations of the Kalman Filter
Edited by Felix Govaers
p. cm.
Print ISBN 978-1-83880-536-4
Online ISBN 978-1-83880-537-1
eBook (PDF) ISBN 978-1-83880-739-9

For EU product safety concerns:
IN TECH d.o.o., Prolaz Marije Krucifikse Kozulić 3, 51000 Rijeka, Croatia, info@intechopen.com or visit our website at intechopen.com.

Meet the editor

Felix Govaers received his Diploma in Mathematics and his PhD with the title "Advanced data fusion in distributed sensor applications" in Computer Science, both from the University of Bonn, Germany. Since 2009 he works at Fraunhofer FKIE in the Department for Sensor Data Fusion and Information Processing where he was leading the research group "Distributed Systems" for three years. Since 2017, he has been the deputy head of the Department for Sensor Data and Information Fusion. Felix Govaers' research is focused on data fusion for state estimation in sensor networks and non-linear filtering. This includes track extraction, processing of delayed measurements, as well as the distributed Kalman filter and track-to-track fusion.

Contents

Preface

Sensor data fusion is the process of combining error-prone, heterogeneous, incomplete, and ambiguous data to gather a higher level of situational awareness. In principle, all living creatures are fusing information from their complementary senses to coordinate their actions and to detect and localize danger. In sensor data fusion, this process is transferred to electronic systems, which rely on some "awareness" of what is happening in certain areas of interest. By means of probability theory and statistics, it is possible to model the relationship between the state space and the sensor data. The number of ingredients of the resulting Kalman filter is limited, but its applications are not.

This book presents recent advances in applications and theory of Kalman filters with a special focus on implementation advice for efficient, fast, and robust state estimation algorithms. These aspects highlight the particular strengths of Kalman filter-based approaches, since the analytical solutions of the Bayes formalism enable smart—and in some way "intelligent"—modifications for lightweight processing algorithms while maintaining data consistency for robustness. This is of great interest for industrial applications such as human assistance systems, robot perception, and advanced driver-assistance systems for automotive platforms due to the constraints in costs, energy, and computational resources.

This book is therefore well suited for practical engineers who are interested in novel techniques for fast and efficient sensor data fusion and non-linear state estimation.

I would like to thank all contributing authors who have made this book possible by sharing their research and empirical knowledge to help others who are building complex systems. Moreover, I would like to thank the forbearing managers at IntechOpen for their support.

Felix Govaers
Fraunhofer FKIE,
Wachtberg, Germany

Section 1

Introduction to the Kalman Filter

Chapter 1

Introductory Chapter: Kalman Filter - The Working Horse of Object Tracking Systems Nowadays

Felix Govaers

1. Introduction

Sensordata fusion is the process of combining error-prone, heterogenous, incomplete, and ambiguous data to gather a higher level of situational awareness. In principle, all living creatures are fusing information from their complementary senses in order to coordinate their actions and to detect and localize danger. In sensor data fusion, this process is transferred to electronic systems, which rely on some "awareness" of what is happening in certain areas of interest, and since the sensors involved most often are confronted with a dynamical world, the state of interest underlies an evolution process in time, which has to be reflected within the data processing. By means of probability theory and statistics, it is possible to model the relationship between the state space and the sensor data. Kinematic laws and stochastic processes further provide the basis for evolution models in object tracking. The number of ingredients of the resulting Kalman filter is limited, but its applications are not.

Invented many decades ago—Kalman's initial paper was published in 1960, and it is well known that similar solutions to the tracking problem were found even earlier—the Kalman filter is an algorithm with an extraordinary career. In the days it was invented, the Kalman filter was designed for tracking airplanes in the sky based on surveillance radars. As a consequence, the problems of measurement error and object dynamics were the key points, which the Kalman filter can cope with. Since then, sensor technology has evolved enormously. In recent decades, sensor technology has become increasingly important for numerous civilian and military applications, and it is obvious that this trend will continue in the future. High performance sensors have conquered many novel applications, and existing applications have been brought to a much higher level of technical complexity. This technological trend is accompanied with an evolution in the field of sensor data processing algorithms. Besides the family of Kalman filters, other solutions to the Bayesian approach to information processing have been developed—based on grids or Monte Carlo simulation for instance. However, the most often used approach for practical tracking system still is the Kalman filter, at least in one of its numerous variants. While the classical assumptions including linear models for sensor and dynamics, perfect data association, and known track existence are mostly handled in the academic and educational field, many extensions have been developed to bring the Kalman filter into practical and industrial systems. It is literally impossible to list all methods that have been developed based on the Kalman filter, a few of the most important variations possibly would be:

- Extended and unscented Kalman filter (EKF/UKF) for nonlinear models.
- Multiple hypothesis tracking (MHT) for ambiguous data association.
- Interacting multiple model (IMM) for Markov Chain motion model systems.
- Distributed Kalman filter (DKF) and information filter for multisensor fusion.
- Random matrix model and hypersurface model for extended target tracking.
- Self-localization and mapping (SLAM) for autonomous navigation in unknown environments.

In the past decade, challenges in target tracking applications have changed again. Today, often heterogenous sensors such as radar, LIDAR, E/O and I/R cameras, and others are combined to achieve robustness and a high level of perception.
Also, Kalman filters are applied to a great variety of applications where, for instance, intelligence data from social media or computer program logs for intrusion detection systems are combined to achieve situational awareness. And, of course, we may not omit the uprising self-driving cars, which might be the most famous application these days. It is a particularly interesting application, since the challenges involved are enormous: bias- and error-prone point clouds are obtained from partially scattering points in the environment, the quality highly depends on weather and daylight conditions, the environment might be unknown, and other participants might not be aware and have to be protected. And all this is safety critical. And the processing unit is supposed to be lightweight for economic reasons.

There are many more examples to demonstrate for further development, trends, and improvements of Kalman filter based algorithms, and I am happy that we have gathered some interest of practical relevance in this book.

2. Kalman filter in the shed light of artificial intelligence

Artificial intelligence (AI) comprises a wide range of technologies and methodologies such as machine learning (ML), support vector machines (SVM), logistic regression (LR), game theory, logic reasoning, and many more. The term was introduced once to highlight the increasing complexity of machines in combination with numerical algorithms for robotic perception for instance. In particular the success in image and video processing based on massive training data, well-tuned models, and high-performance hardware has created a boost in research and expectations for new AI applications and results in the past years. ML methods show good performances when it comes to perception task such as object classification and image segmentation; however, it will be hard to match the expectations on AI if models created and tested by engineers together with logic reasoning and the Bayes formalism are kept out of complex systems with decision-making and strategic situational awareness on a higher level. This is due to the fact that ML encodes correlations between input data and the resulting class very efficiently but does not have a concept to infer causality. Thus, a deeper understanding beyond a rough comparison of shallow features is not possible. But often, this is not enough. In particular when it comes to safety critical applications or even military use, a mere performance argument is not sufficient to justify the usage of algorithms, which still suffer from the black box property with respect to the transparency of computed results. Moreover, one cannot overemphasize the dependency of ML methods on huge training sequences, which must be labeled for most useful applications. Image recognition essentially is solved due to the fact that there are tons of labeled pictures in the Internet. However, this is not the case for complex multisensor systems, which must adapt appropriately in unseen environments. Moreover, it is obvious that the feature space grows exponentially when it comes to complex systems and higher-order reasoning. As a consequence, the amount of data which would be necessary to train a neural network for such systems is a natural show stopper. This is where we will find logic reasoning and Bayes methods such as the Kalman filters (KF) increasingly. The human experience and ability to infer chains of causality can be transferred into AI algorithms by means of sensor models, motion models, and time evolution models. The KF with its low weight consumption when it comes to numerical costs is an important backbone in advanced driver assistance systems already, and this trend is about to continue heavily.

Author details

Felix Govaers
Fraunhofer FKIE, Wachtberg, Germany

*Address all correspondence to: felix.govaers@fkie.fraunhofer.de

Chapter 2

Introduction to Kalman Filter and Its Applications

Youngjoo Kim and Hyochoong Bang

Abstract

We provide a tutorial-like description of Kalman filter and extended Kalman filter. This chapter aims for those who need to teach Kalman filters to others, or for those who do not have a strong background in estimation theory. Following a problem definition of state estimation, filtering algorithms will be presented with supporting examples to help readers easily grasp how the Kalman filters work. Implementations on INS/GNSS navigation, target tracking, and terrain-referenced navigation (TRN) are given. In each example, we discuss how to choose, implement, tune, and modify the algorithms for real world practices. Source codes for implementing the examples are also provided. In conclusion, this chapter will become a prerequisite for other contents in the book.

Keywords: Kalman filter, extended Kalman filter, INS/GNSS navigation, target tracking, terrain-referenced navigation

1. Introduction

Kalman filtering is an algorithm that provides estimates of some unknown variables given the measurements observed over time. Kalman filters have been demonstrating its usefulness in various applications. Kalman filters have relatively simple form and require small computational power. However, it is still not easy for people who are not familiar with estimation theory to understand and implement the Kalman filters. Whereas there exist some excellent literatures such as [1] addressing derivation and theory behind the Kalman filter, this chapter focuses on a more practical perspective.

Following two chapters will devote to introduce algorithms of Kalman filter and extended Kalman filter, respectively, including their applications. With linear models with additive Gaussian noises, the Kalman filter provides optimal estimates. Navigation with a global navigation satellite system (GNSS) will be provided as an implementation example of the Kalman filter. The extended Kalman filter is utilized for nonlinear problems like bearing-angle target tracking and terrain-referenced navigation (TRN). How to implement the filtering algorithms for such applications will be presented in detail.

2. Kalman filter

2.1 Problem definition

Kalman filters are used to estimate states based on linear dynamical systems in state space format. The process model defines the evolution of the state from time $k-1$ to time k as:

$$\boldsymbol{x}_k = F\boldsymbol{x}_{k-1} + B\boldsymbol{u}_{k-1} + \boldsymbol{w}_{k-1} \tag{1}$$

where F is the state transition matrix applied to the previous state vector $\boldsymbol{x}_{k-1}$, B is the control-input matrix applied to the control vector $\boldsymbol{u}_{k-1}$, and $\boldsymbol{w}_{k-1}$ is the process noise vector that is assumed to be zero-mean Gaussian with the covariance Q, i.e., $\boldsymbol{w}_{k-1} \sim \mathcal{N}(0, Q)$.

The process model is paired with the measurement model that describes the relationship between the state and the measurement at the current time step k as:

$$\mathbf{z}_k = H\boldsymbol{x}_k + \boldsymbol{\nu}_k \tag{2}$$

where $\mathbf{z}_k$ is the measurement vector, H is the measurement matrix, and $\boldsymbol{\nu}_k$ is the measurement noise vector that is assumed to be zero-mean Gaussian with the covariance R, i.e., $\boldsymbol{\nu}_k \sim \mathcal{N}(0, R)$. Note that sometimes the term "measurement" is called "observation" in different literature.

The role of the Kalman filter is to provide estimate of $\boldsymbol{x}_k$ at time k, given the initial estimate of $\boldsymbol{x}_0$, the series of measurement, $\mathbf{z}_1, \mathbf{z}_2, \ldots, \mathbf{z}_k$, and the information of the system described by F, B, H, Q, and R. Note that subscripts to these matrices are omitted here by assuming that they are invariant over time as in most applications. Although the covariance matrices are supposed to reflect the statistics of the noises, the true statistics of the noises is not known or not Gaussian in many practical applications. Therefore, Q and R are usually used as tuning parameters that the user can adjust to get desired performance.

2.2 Kalman filter algorithm

Kalman filter algorithm consists of two stages: prediction and update. Note that the terms "prediction" and "update" are often called "propagation" and "correction," respectively, in different literature. The Kalman filter algorithm is summarized as follows:

Prediction:

Predicted state estimate	$\hat{\boldsymbol{x}}_k^- = F\hat{\boldsymbol{x}}_{k-1}^+ + B\boldsymbol{u}_{k-1}$
Predicted error covariance	$P_k^- = FP_{k-1}^+F^T + Q$

Update:

Measurement residual	$\tilde{\boldsymbol{y}}_k = \mathbf{z}_k - H\hat{\boldsymbol{x}}_k^-$
Kalman gain	$K_k = P_k^-H^T\left(R + HP_k^-H^T\right)^{-1}$
Updated state estimate	$\hat{\boldsymbol{x}}_k^+ = \hat{\boldsymbol{x}}_k^- + K_k\tilde{\boldsymbol{y}}$
Updated error covariance	$P_k^+ = (I - K_kH)P_k^-$

In the above equations, the hat operator, ^, means an estimate of a variable. That is, $\hat{\boldsymbol{x}}$ is an estimate of $\boldsymbol{x}$. The superscripts – and + denote predicted (prior) and updated (posterior) estimates, respectively.

The predicted state estimate is evolved from the updated previous updated state estimate. The new term P is called state error covariance. It encrypts the error covariance that the filter thinks the estimate error has. Note that the covariance of a random variable $\boldsymbol{x}$ is defined as $\text{cov}(\boldsymbol{x}) = \mathbb{E}\left[(\boldsymbol{x} - \hat{\boldsymbol{x}})(\boldsymbol{x} - \hat{\boldsymbol{x}})^T\right]^T$ where $\mathbb{E}$ denotes the expected (mean) value of its argument. One can observe that the error covariance becomes larger at the prediction stage due to the summation with Q, which means the filter is more uncertain of the state estimate after the prediction step.

In the update stage, the measurement residual $\widetilde{\boldsymbol{y}}_k$ is computed first. The measurement residual, also known as innovation, is the difference between the true measurement, $\mathbf{z}_k$, and the estimated measurement, $H\hat{\boldsymbol{x}}_k^-$. The filter estimates the current measurement by multiplying the predicted state by the measurement matrix. The residual, $\widetilde{\boldsymbol{y}}_k$, is later then multiplied by the Kalman gain, K_k, to provide the correction, $K_k\widetilde{\boldsymbol{y}}_\text{k}$, to the predicted estimate $\hat{\boldsymbol{x}}_k^-$. After it obtains the updated state estimate, the Kalman filter calculates the updated error covariance, P_k^+, which will be used in the next time step. Note that the updated error covariance is smaller than the predicted error covariance, which means the filter is more certain of the state estimate after the measurement is utilized in the update stage.

We need an initialization stage to implement the Kalman filter. As initial values, we need the initial guess of state estimate, $\hat{\boldsymbol{x}}_0^+$, and the initial guess of the error covariance matrix, P_0^+. Together with Q and R, $\hat{\boldsymbol{x}}_0^+$ and P_0^+ play an important role to obtain desired performance. There is a rule of thumb called "initial ignorance," which means that the user should choose a large P_0^+ for quicker convergence. Finally, one can obtain implement a Kalman filter by implementing the prediction and update stages for each time step, $k = 1, 2, 3, \ldots$, after the initialization of estimates.

Note that Kalman filters are derived based on the assumption that the process and measurement models are linear, i.e., they can be expressed with the matrices F, B, and H, and the process and measurement noise are additive Gaussian. Hence, a Kalman filter provides optimal estimate only if the assumptions are satisfied.

2.3 Example

An example for implementing the Kalman filter is navigation where the vehicle state, position, and velocity are estimated by using sensor output from an inertial measurement unit (IMU) and a global navigation satellite system (GNSS) receiver. In this example, we consider only position and velocity, omitting attitude information. The three-dimensional position and velocity comprise the state vector:

$$\boldsymbol{x} = \left[\boldsymbol{p}^T, \boldsymbol{v}^T\right]^T \tag{3}$$

where $\boldsymbol{p} = \left[p_x, p_y, p_z\right]^T$ is the position vector and $\boldsymbol{v} = \left[v_x, v_y, v_z\right]^T$ is the velocity vector whose elements are defined in x, y, z axes. The state in time k can be predicted by the previous state in time $k - 1$ as:

$$\boldsymbol{x}_k = \begin{bmatrix} \boldsymbol{p}_k \\ \boldsymbol{v}_k \end{bmatrix} = \begin{bmatrix} \boldsymbol{p}_{k-1} + \boldsymbol{v}_{k-1}\Delta t + \frac{1}{2}\widetilde{\boldsymbol{a}}_{k-1}\Delta t^2 \\ \boldsymbol{v}_{k-1} + \widetilde{\boldsymbol{a}}_{k-1}\Delta t \end{bmatrix} \tag{4}$$

where $\tilde{\boldsymbol{a}}_{k-1}$ is the acceleration applied to the vehicle. The above equation can be rearranged as:

$$\boldsymbol{x}_k = \begin{bmatrix} I_{3\times3} & I_{3\times3}\Delta t \\ 0_{3\times3} & I_{3\times3} \end{bmatrix} \boldsymbol{x}_{k-1} + \begin{bmatrix} \frac{1}{2} I_{3\times3}\Delta t^2 \\ I_{3\times3}\Delta t \end{bmatrix} \tilde{\boldsymbol{a}}_{k-1} \tag{5}$$

where $I_{3\times3}$ and $0_{3\times3}$ denote 3×3 identity and zero matrices, respectively. The process noise comes from the accelerometer output, $\boldsymbol{a}_{k-1} = \tilde{\boldsymbol{a}}_{k-1} + \boldsymbol{e}_{k-1}$, where $\boldsymbol{e}_{k-1}$ denotes the noise of the accelerometer output. Suppose $\boldsymbol{e}_{k-1} \sim \mathcal{N}\left(0, I_{3\times3}\sigma_e^2\right)$. From the covariance relationship, $\text{Cov}(A\boldsymbol{x}) = A\Sigma A^T$ where $\text{Cov}(\boldsymbol{x}) = \Sigma$, we get the covariance matrix of the process noise as:

$$Q = \begin{bmatrix} \frac{1}{2} I_{3\times3}\Delta t^2 \\ I_{3\times3}\Delta t \end{bmatrix} I_{3\times3}\sigma_e^2 \begin{bmatrix} \frac{1}{2} I_{3\times3}\Delta t^2 \\ I_{3\times3}\Delta t \end{bmatrix}^T = \begin{bmatrix} \frac{1}{4} I_{3\times3}\Delta t^4 & 0_{3\times3} \\ 0_{3\times3} & I_{3\times3}\Delta t^2 \end{bmatrix} \sigma_e^2 \tag{6}$$

Now, we have the process model as:

$$\boldsymbol{x}_k = F\boldsymbol{x}_{k-1} + B\boldsymbol{a}_{k-1} + \boldsymbol{w}_{k-1} \tag{7}$$

where

$$F = \begin{bmatrix} I_{3\times3} & I_{3\times3}\Delta t \\ 0_{3\times3} & I_{3\times3} \end{bmatrix} \tag{8}$$

$$B = \begin{bmatrix} \frac{1}{2} I_{3\times3}\Delta t^2 \\ I_{3\times3}\Delta t \end{bmatrix} \tag{9}$$

$$\boldsymbol{w}_{k-1} \sim \mathcal{N}(0, Q) \tag{10}$$

The GNSS receiver provides position and velocity measurements corrupted by measurement noise $\boldsymbol{\nu}_k$ as:

$$\boldsymbol{z}_k = \begin{bmatrix} \boldsymbol{p}_k \\ \boldsymbol{v}_k \end{bmatrix} + \boldsymbol{\nu}_k \tag{11}$$

It is straightforward to derive the measurement model as:

$$\boldsymbol{z}_k = H\boldsymbol{x}_k + \boldsymbol{\nu}_k \tag{12}$$

where

$$H = I_{6\times6} \tag{13}$$

$$\boldsymbol{\nu}_k \sim \mathcal{N}(0, R) \tag{14}$$

In order to conduct a simulation to see how it works, let us consider $N = 20$ time steps ($k = 1, 2, 3, \ldots, N$) with $\Delta t = 1$. It is recommended to generate a time history of true state, or a true trajectory, first. The most convenient way is to generate the series of true accelerations over time and integrate them to get true velocity and position. In this example, the true acceleration is set to zero and the vehicle is moving with a constant velocity, $\boldsymbol{v}_k = [5, 5, 0]^T$ for all $k = 1, 2, 3, \ldots, N$, from the initial position, $\boldsymbol{p}_0 = [0, 0, 0]$. Note that one who uses the Kalman filter to estimate the vehicle state is usually not aware whether the vehicle has a constant velocity or not. This case is not different from nonzero acceleration case in perspective of this Kalman filter models. If the filter designer (you) has some prior knowledge of the vehicle maneuver, process models can be designed in different forms for best describing various maneuvers as in [2].

We need to generate noise of acceleration output and GNSS measurements for every time step. Suppose the acceleration output, GNSS position, and GNSS velocity are corrupted with noise with variances of 0.3^2, 3^2, and 0.03^2, respectively. For each axis, one can use MATLAB function randn or normrnd for generating the Gaussian noise.

The process noise covariance matrix, Q, and measurement noise covariance matrix, R, can be constructed following the real noise statistics described above to get the best performance. However, have in mind that in real applications, we do not know the real statistics of the noises and the noises are often not Gaussian. Common practice is to conservatively set Q and R slightly larger than the expected values to get robustness.

Let us start filtering with the initial guesses

$$\hat{\boldsymbol{x}}_0^+ = [2, -2, 0, 5, 5.1, 0.1]^T \tag{15}$$

$$P_0^+ = \begin{bmatrix} I_{3\times3}4^2 & 0_{3\times3} \\ 0_{3\times3} & I_{3\times3}0.4^2 \end{bmatrix} \tag{16}$$

and noise covariance matrices

$$Q = \begin{bmatrix} \frac{1}{4} I_{3\times3}\Delta t^4 & 0_{3\times3} \\ 0_{3\times3} & I_{3\times3}\Delta t^2 \end{bmatrix} 0.3^2 \tag{17}$$

$$R = \begin{bmatrix} I_{3\times3}3^2 & 0_{3\times3} \\ 0_{3\times3} & I_{3\times3}0.03^2 \end{bmatrix} \tag{18}$$

where Q and R are constant for every time step. The more uncertain your initial guess for the state is, the larger the initial error covariance should be.

In this simulation, $M = 100$ Monte-Carlo runs were conducted. A single run is not sufficient for verifying the statistic characteristic of the filtering result because each sample of a noise differs whenever the noise is sampled from a given distribution, and therefore, every simulation run results in different state estimate. The repetitive Monte-Carlo runs enable us to test a number of different noise samples for each time step.

The time history of estimation errors of two Monte-Carlo runs is depicted in **Figure 1**. We observe that the estimation results of different simulation runs are different even if the initial guess for the state estimate is the same. You can also run the Monte-Carlo simulation with different initial guesses (sampled from a distribution) for the state estimate.

The standard deviation of the estimation errors and the estimated standard deviation for x-axis position and velocity are drawn in **Figure 2**. The standard deviation of the estimation error, or the root mean square error (RMSE), can be obtained by computing standard deviation of M estimation errors for each time step. The estimated standard deviation was obtained by taking squared root of the

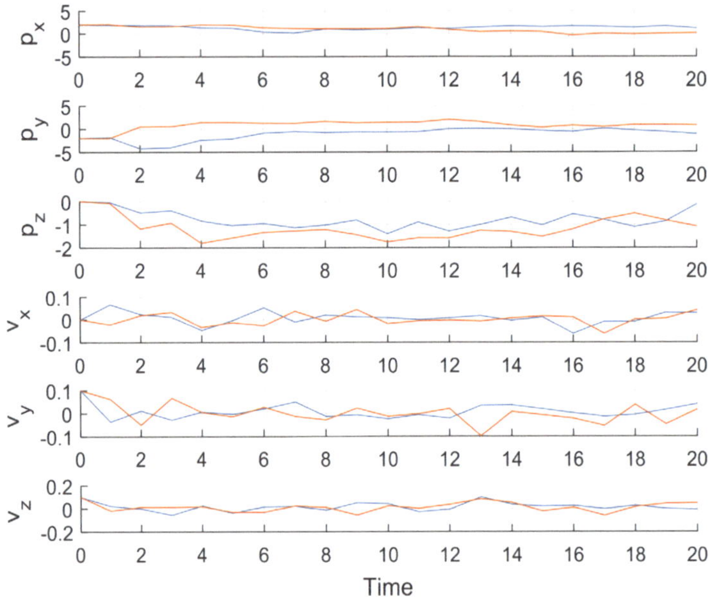

Figure 1.
Time history of estimation errors.

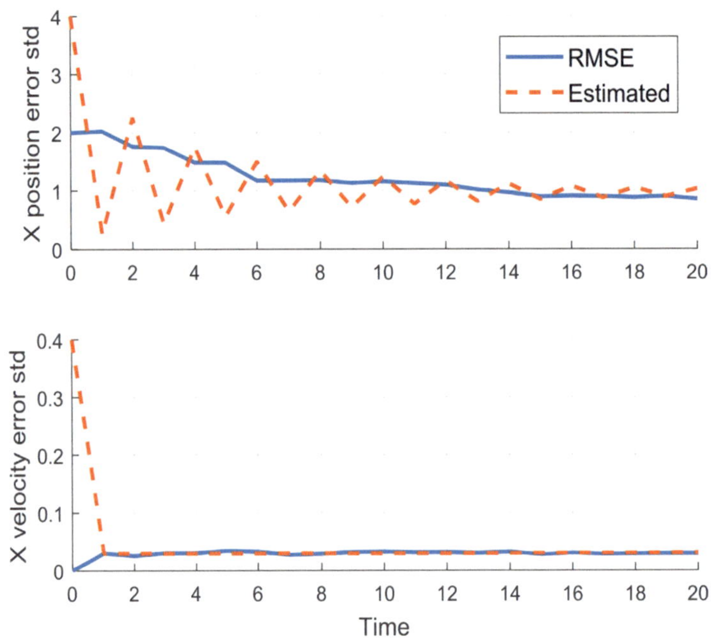

Figure 2.
Actual and estimated standard deviation for x-axis estimate errors.

corresponding diagonal term of P_k^+. Drawing the estimated standard deviation for each axis is possible because the state estimates are independent to each other in this example. A care is needed if P_k^+ has nonzero off-diagonal terms. The estimated standard deviation and the actual standard deviation of estimate errors are very similar. In this case, the filter is called consistent. Note that the estimated error covariance matrix is affected solely by P_0^+, Q, and R, judging from the Kalman filter algorithm. Different settings to these matrices will result in different P_k^+ and therefore different state estimates.

In real applications, you will be able to acquire only the estimated covariance because you will hardly have a chance to conduct Monte-Carlo runs. Also, getting a good estimate of Q and R is often difficult. One practical approach to estimate the noise covariance matirces is the autocovariance least-squares (ALS) technique [3] or an adaptive Kalman filter where the noise covariance matrices are adjusted in real time can be used [4].

Source code of MATLAB implementation for this example can be found in [5]. It is recommended for the readers to change the parameters and aircraft trajectory by yourself and see what happens.

3. Extended Kalman filter

3.1 Problem definition

Suppose you have a nonlinear dynamic system where you are not able to define either the process model or measurement model with multiplication of vectors and matrices as in (1) and (2). The extended Kalman filter provides us a tool for dealing with such nonlinear models in an efficient way. Since it is computationally cheaper than other nonlinear filtering methods such as point-mass filters and particle filters, the extended Kalman filter has been used in various real-time applications like navigation systems.

The extended Kalman filter can be viewed as a nonlinear version of the Kalman filter that linearized the models about a current estimate. Suppose we have the following models for state transition and measurement

$$\boldsymbol{x}_k = \boldsymbol{f}(\boldsymbol{x}_{k-1}, \boldsymbol{u}_{k-1}) + \boldsymbol{w}_{k-1} \tag{19}$$

$$\boldsymbol{z}_k = \boldsymbol{h}(\boldsymbol{x}_k) + \boldsymbol{\nu}_k \tag{20}$$

where $\boldsymbol{f}$ is the function of the previous state, $\boldsymbol{x}_{k-1}$, and the control input, $\boldsymbol{u}_{k-1}$, that provides the current state $\boldsymbol{x}_k$. $\boldsymbol{h}$ is the measurement function that relates the current state, $\boldsymbol{x}_k$, to the measurement $\boldsymbol{z}_k$. $\boldsymbol{w}_{k-1}$ and $\boldsymbol{\nu}_k$ are Gaussian noises for the process model and the measurement model with covariance Q and R, respectively.

3.2. Extended Kalman filter algorithm

All you need is to obtain the Jacobian matrix, first-order partial derivative of a vector function with respect to a vector, of each model in each time step as:

$$F_{k-1} = \left.\frac{\partial \boldsymbol{f}}{\partial \boldsymbol{x}}\right|_{\hat{\boldsymbol{x}}_{k-1}^{+}, \boldsymbol{u}_{k-1}} \tag{21}$$

$$H_k = \left.\frac{\partial \boldsymbol{h}}{\partial \boldsymbol{x}}\right|_{\hat{\boldsymbol{x}}_k^{-}} \tag{22}$$

Note the subscripts of F and H are maintained here since the matrices are often varying with different values of the state vector for each time step. By doing this, you linearize the models about the current estimate. The filter algorithm is very similar to Kalman filter.

Prediction:

Predicted state estimate	$\hat{\boldsymbol{x}}_k^- = \boldsymbol{f}(\hat{\boldsymbol{x}}_{k-1}^+, \boldsymbol{u}_{k-1})$
Predicted error covariance	$P_k^- = F_{k-1}P_{k-1}^+F_{k-1}^T + Q$

Update:

Measurement residual	$\tilde{\boldsymbol{y}}_k = \boldsymbol{z}_k - \boldsymbol{h}(\hat{\boldsymbol{x}}_k^-)$
Kalman gain	$K_k = P_k^- H_k^T (R + H_k P_k^- H_k^T)^{-1}$
Updated state estimate	$\hat{\boldsymbol{x}}_k^+ = \hat{\boldsymbol{x}}_k^- + K_k \tilde{\boldsymbol{y}}$
Updated error covariance	$P_k^+ = (I - K_k H_k) P_k^-$

As in the Kalman filter algorithm, the hat operator, ^, means an estimate of a variable. That is, $\hat{\boldsymbol{x}}$ is an estimate of $\boldsymbol{x}$. The superscripts – and + denote predicted (prior) and updated (posterior) estimates, respectively. The main difference from the Kalman filter is that the extended Kalman filter obtains predicted state estimate and predicted measurement by the nonlinear functions $\boldsymbol{f}(\boldsymbol{x}_{k-1}, \boldsymbol{u}_{k-1})$ and $\boldsymbol{h}(\boldsymbol{x}_k)$, respectively.

3.3 Example

3.3.1 Target tracking

We are going to estimate a 3-dimensional target state (position and velocity) by using measurements provided by a range sensor and an angle sensor. For example, a radar system can provide range and angle measurement and a combination of a camera and a rangefinder can do the same. We define the target state as:

$$\boldsymbol{x} = \left[\boldsymbol{p}^T, \boldsymbol{v}^T\right]^T \tag{23}$$

where $\boldsymbol{p}$ and $\boldsymbol{v}$ denote position and velocity of the target, respectively. The system model is described as a near-constant-velocity model [2] in discrete time space by:

$$\boldsymbol{x}_k = \begin{bmatrix} \boldsymbol{p}_k \\ \boldsymbol{v}_k \end{bmatrix} = \boldsymbol{f}(\boldsymbol{x}_{k-1}, \boldsymbol{u}_{k-1}) = \begin{bmatrix} \boldsymbol{p}_{k-1} + \boldsymbol{v}_{k-1}\Delta t \\ \boldsymbol{v}_{k-1} \end{bmatrix} + \boldsymbol{w}_{k-1} \tag{24}$$

The process noise has the covariance of $\boldsymbol{w}_{k-1} \sim \mathcal{N}(0, Q)$ where

$$Q = \begin{bmatrix} 0_{3\times3} & 0_{3\times3} \\ 0_{3\times3} & \begin{matrix} \sigma_x^2 & 0 & 0 \\ 0 & \sigma_y^2 & 0 \\ 0 & 0 & \sigma_z^2 \end{matrix} \end{bmatrix} \tag{25}$$

and σ_x, σ_y, and σ_z are the standard deviations of the process noise on the velocity in x, y, and z directions, respectively.

The measurement vector is composed of line-of-sight angles to the target, $\mathcal{A}$ and $\mathcal{E}$, and the range, $\mathcal{R}$, to the target. The relationship between the measurement and the relative target state with respect to the sensor comprises the measurement model as:

$$\mathbf{z}_k = \begin{bmatrix} \mathcal{A} \\ \mathcal{E} \\ \mathcal{R} \end{bmatrix} = \boldsymbol{h}(\boldsymbol{x}_k) = \begin{bmatrix} atan\left(\dfrac{x_t - x_s}{y_t - y_s}\right) \\ atan\left(\dfrac{\mathbf{z}_t - \mathbf{z}_s}{\sqrt{(x_t - x_s)^2 + (y_t - y_s)^2}}\right) \\ \sqrt{(x_t - x_s)^2 + (y_t - y_s)^2 + (\mathbf{z}_t - \mathbf{z}_s)^2} \end{bmatrix} + \boldsymbol{\nu}_k \qquad (26)$$

where $p_k = [x_t, y_t, \mathbf{z}_t]^T$ is the position vector of the target and $[x_s, y_s, \mathbf{z}_s]^T$ is the position vector of the sensor. The target position is the variable in this measurement model. Note that the measurement has nonlinear relationship with the target state. This cannot be expressed in a matrix form as in (2) whereas the process model can be. If at least one model is nonlinear, we should use nonlinear filtering technique. In order to apply extended Kalman filter to this problem, let us take first derivatives of the process model and measurement model as:

$$F_{k-1} = \left.\frac{\partial \boldsymbol{f}}{\partial \boldsymbol{x}}\right|_{\hat{\boldsymbol{x}}^+_{k-1}, \boldsymbol{u}_{k-1}} = \begin{bmatrix} I_{3\times3} & I_{3\times3}\Delta t \\ 0_{3\times3} & I_{3\times3} \end{bmatrix} \qquad (27)$$

$$H_k = \left.\frac{\partial \boldsymbol{h}}{\partial \boldsymbol{x}}\right|_{\hat{\boldsymbol{x}}^-_k} = \begin{bmatrix} \dfrac{y}{x^2+y^2} & \dfrac{-x}{x^2+y^2} & 0 & \\ \dfrac{-x\mathbf{z}}{(x^2+y^2+\mathbf{z}^2)\sqrt{x^2+y^2}} & \dfrac{-y\mathbf{z}}{(x^2+y^2+\mathbf{z}^2)\sqrt{x^2+y^2}} & \dfrac{1}{\sqrt{x^2+y^2}} & 0_{3\times3} \\ \dfrac{x}{\sqrt{x^2+y^2+\mathbf{z}^2}} & \dfrac{y}{\sqrt{x^2+y^2+\mathbf{z}^2}} & \dfrac{\mathbf{z}}{\sqrt{x^2+y^2+\mathbf{z}^2}} & \end{bmatrix} \qquad (28)$$

where $[x, y, \mathbf{z}]^T = [x_t - x_s, y_t - y_s, \mathbf{z}_t - \mathbf{z}_s]^T$ is the relative position vector. Note that the matrix H_k varies with different values of $[x, y, \mathbf{z}]^T$ on which the filtering result will, therefore, depend. Thus, one can plan the trajectory of the sensor to get a better filtering result [6]. Developing such a method is one of active research topics.

In the simulation, the sensor is initially located at $[x_s, y_s, \mathbf{z}_s]^T = [40, 20, 50]^T$ and the sensor is moving in a circular pattern with a radius of 20 centered at $[20, 20, 50]^T$. The initial state of the target is $\boldsymbol{x}_0 = [10, -10, 0, -1, -2, 0]^T$. The sensor is moving with a constant velocity of $[-1, -2, 0]^T$. The trajectory of the target and the sensor is shown in **Figure 3**. Note that this is the case where we are aware that the target has a constant velocity, unlike the example in Section 2.3, which is why we modeled the state transition as the near-constant-velocity model in (4). Let us consider $N = 20$ time steps ($k = 1, 2, 3, \ldots, N$) with $\Delta t = 1$. Suppose the measurements are corrupted with a Gaussian noise whose standard deviation is $[0.02, 0.02, 1.0]^T$.

In the filter side, the covariance matrix for the process noise can be set as:

$$Q = \begin{bmatrix} 0_{3\times3} & 0_{3\times3} \\ 0_{3\times3} & I_{3\times3}\sigma_v^2 \end{bmatrix} \qquad (29)$$

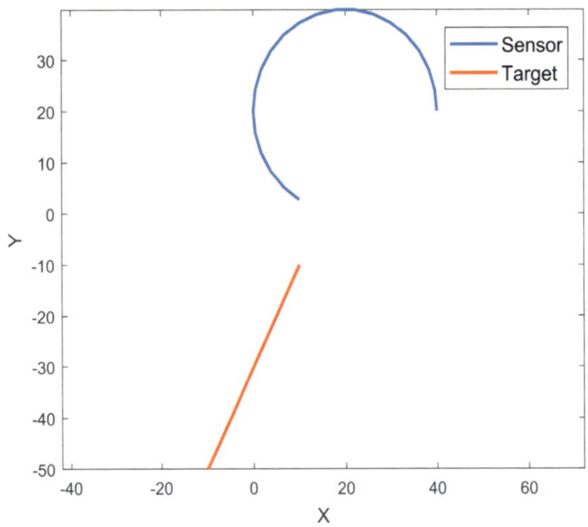

Figure 3.
Trajectory of the sensor and the target.

where $\sigma_v = 5$ is the tuning parameter that denotes how uncertain the velocity estimate is. The measurement covariance matrix was constructed following the real noise statistics as:

$$R = \begin{bmatrix} 0.02^2 & 0 & 0 \\ 0 & 0.02^2 & 0 \\ 0 & 0 & 1.0^2 \end{bmatrix} \tag{30}$$

$M = 100$ Monte-Carlo runs were conducted with the following initial guesses:

$$\hat{\boldsymbol{x}}_0^+ = \boldsymbol{x}_0 + \text{normrnd}(0, [1, 1, 0, 0, 0, 0]) \tag{31}$$

$$P_0^+ = \begin{bmatrix} I_{3\times3}1^2 & 0_{3\times3} \\ 0_{3\times3} & I_{3\times3}0.1^2 \end{bmatrix} \tag{32}$$

The above equation means that the error of the initial guess for the target state is randomly sampled from a Gaussian distribution with a standard deviation of $[1, 1, 0, 0, 0, 0]$.

Time history of an estimation result for x-axis position and velocity is drawn together with the true value in **Figure 4**. The shape of the line will be different at each run. The statistical result can be shown as **Figure 5**. Note that the filter worked inconsistently with the estimated error covariance different from the actual value. This is because the process error covariance is set to a very large number. In this example, the large process error covariance is the only choice a user can make because the measurement cannot correct the velocity. One can notice that the measurement Eq. (26) has no term dependent on the velocity, and therefore, matrix H in (28) has zero elements on the right side of the matrix where the derivatives of the measurement equation with respect to velocity are located. As a result, the measurement residual has no effect on velocity correction. In this case, we say the system has no observability on velocity. In practice, this problem can be mitigated by setting the process noise covariance to a large number so that the filter believes the measurement is more reliable. In this way, we can prevent at least the position estimate from diverging.

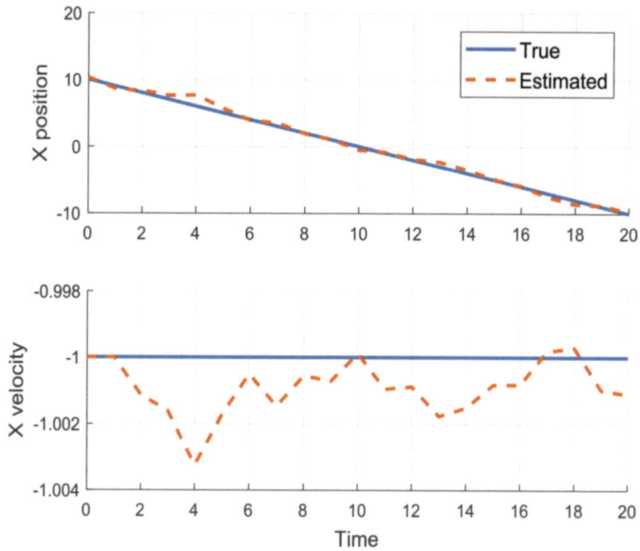

Figure 4.
Time history of an estimation result for x-axis position and velocity.

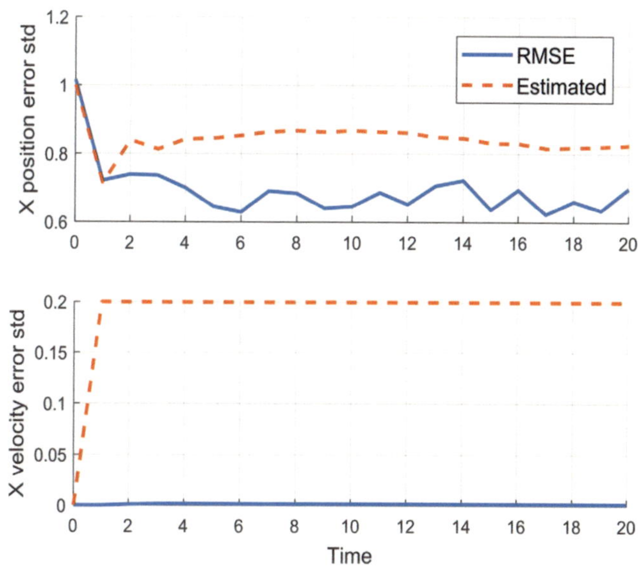

Figure 5.
Actual and estimated standard deviation for x axis estimate errors.

Source code of MATLAB implementation for this example can be found in [5]. It is recommended for the readers to change the parameters and trajectories by yourself and see what happens.

3.3.2 Terrain-referenced navigation

Terrain-referenced navigation (TRN), also known as terrain-aided navigation (TAN), provides positioning data by comparing terrain measurements with a digital elevation model (DEM) stored on an on-board computer of an aircraft. The TRN algorithm blends a navigational solution from an inertial navigation system (INS) with the measured terrain profile underneath the aircraft. Terrain measurements have generally been obtained by using radar altimeters. TRN systems using cameras [7], airborne laser sensors [8], and interferometric radar altimeters [9] have also been addressed. Unlike GNSS's, TRN systems are resistant to electronic jamming and interference, and are able to operate in a wide range of weather conditions. Thus, TRN systems are expected to be alternative/supplement systems to GNSS's.

The movement of the aircraft is modeled by the following Markov process:

$$\boldsymbol{x}_k = \boldsymbol{x}_{k-1} + \boldsymbol{u}_{k-1} + \boldsymbol{w}_{k-1} \tag{33}$$

where $\boldsymbol{x}_{k-1}$, $\boldsymbol{u}_{k-1}$, and $\boldsymbol{w}_{k-1}$ denote the state vector, the relative movement, and the additive Gaussian process noise, respectively, at time $k-1$. $\boldsymbol{x}_k = [\phi, \lambda]^T$ is a two-dimensional state vector, which denotes the aircraft's horizontal position. Estimates of the relative movement (velocity) are provided by the INS and their error is absorbed into $\boldsymbol{w}_{k-1}$ to limit the dimensionality of the state. The simple model in (33) is considered realistic without details of INS integration if an independent attitude solution is available so that the velocity can be resolved in an earth-fixed frame [10]. The estimation models we deal with belong to the TRN filter block in **Figure 6**, taking relative movement information from the INS as $\boldsymbol{u}_k$.

Typical TRN systems utilize measurements of the terrain elevation underneath an aircraft. The terrain elevation measurement is modeled as:

$$\mathbf{z}_k = h(\boldsymbol{x}_k) + v_k \tag{34}$$

where $h(\boldsymbol{x}_k)$ denotes terrain elevation from the DEM evaluated at the horizontal position, $\boldsymbol{x}_k$, and v_k denotes the additive Gaussian measurement noise. The elevation measurement is obtained by subtracting the ground clearance measurement from a radar altimeter, h_r, from the barometric altimeter measurement, h_b. v_k contains errors of the radar altimeter, barometric altimeter, and DEM. The ground clearance and the barometric altitude correspond to the above ground level (AGL) height and the mean sea level (MSL) height, respectively. The relationship between the measurements is depicted in **Figure 7**. Note that the terrain elevation that comprises the measurement model in (34) is highly nonlinear.

The process model in (33) and the measurement model in (34) can be linearized as:

$$F_{k-1} = \left.\frac{\partial f}{\partial \boldsymbol{x}}\right|_{\hat{\boldsymbol{x}}^+_{k-1},\, \boldsymbol{u}_{k-1}} = I_{2\times 2} \tag{35}$$

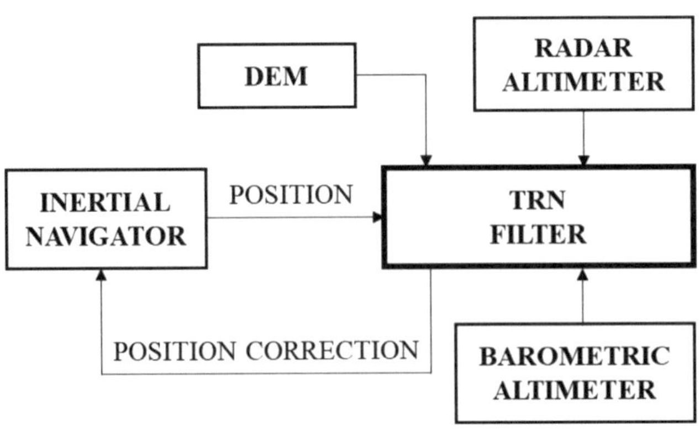

Figure 6.
Conventional TRN structure.

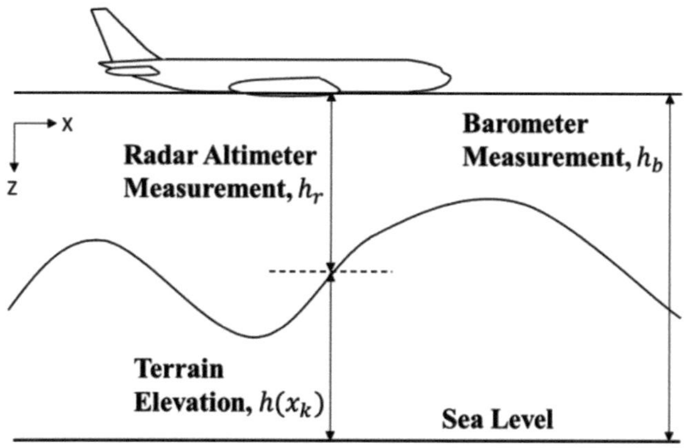

Figure 7.
Relationship between measurements in TRN.

$$H_k = \left.\frac{\partial h}{\partial \boldsymbol{x}}\right|_{\hat{x}_k^-} = \begin{bmatrix} \dfrac{\partial D(\phi,\lambda)}{\partial \phi} & \dfrac{\partial D(\phi,\lambda)}{\partial \lambda} \end{bmatrix} \tag{36}$$

where $D(\phi, \lambda)$ denotes the terrain elevation from the DEM on the horizontal position $[\phi, \lambda]^T$.

The DEMs are essentially provided as matrices containing grid-spaced elevation data. For obtaining finer-resolution data, interpolation techniques are often used to estimate the unknown value in between the grid points. One of the simplest methods is linear interpolation. Linear interpolation is quick and easy, but it is not very precise. A generalization of linear interpolation is polynomial interpolation. Polynomial interpolation expresses data points as higher degree polynomial. Polynomial interpolation overcomes most of the problems of linear interpolation. However, calculating the interpolating polynomial is computationally expensive. Furthermore, the shape of the resulting curve may be different to what is known about the data, especially for very high or low values of the independent variable. These disadvantages can be resolved by using spline interpolation. Spline interpolation uses low-degree polynomials in each of the data intervals and let the polynomial pieces fit smoothly together. That is, its second derivative is zero at the grid points (see [11] for more details). Classical approach to use polynomials of degree 3 is called cubic spline. Because the elevation data are contained in a two-dimensional array, bilinear or bicubic interpolation are generally used. Interpolation for two-dimensional gridded data can be realized by interp2 function in MATLAB. Cubic spline interpolation is used in this example.

The DEM we are using in this example has a 100×100 grid with a resolution of 30. The profile of the DEM can be depicted as **Figure 8**. The figure represents contours of the terrain where brighter color denotes regions with higher altitude. The point (20, 10) in the grid corresponds to the position $[600, 300]^T$ in the navigation frame.

An aircraft, initially located at $\boldsymbol{x}_0 = [400, 400]^T$, is moving by 20 every time step in x direction. The aircraft is equipped with a radar altimter and a barometric altimter, which are used for obtaining the terrain elevation. This measured terrain elevation is compared to the DEM to estimate the vehicle's position.

The process noise $\boldsymbol{w}_{k-1}$ is a zero-mean Gaussian noise with the standard deviation of $[0.5, 0.5]^T$. The radar altimeter is corrupted with a zero-mean Gaussian noise

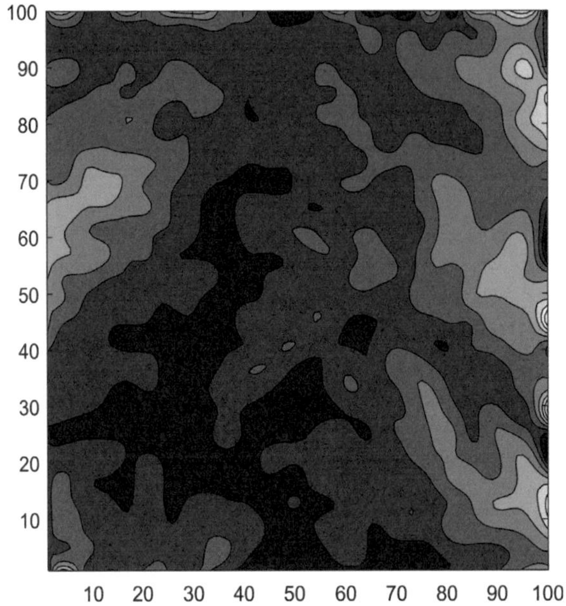

Figure 8.
Contour representation of terrain profile.

with the standard deviation of 3. The matrices Q and R are following the real statistics of the noises as:

$$Q = \begin{bmatrix} 0.5^2 & 0 \\ 0 & 0.5^2 \end{bmatrix} \tag{37}$$

$$R = 3^2 \tag{38}$$

Let us consider $N = 100$ time steps ($k = 1, 2, 3, \ldots, N$) with $\Delta t = 1$. $M = 100$ Monte-Carlo runs were conducted with the following initial guesses:

$$\hat{\boldsymbol{x}}_0^+ = \boldsymbol{x}_0 + \text{normrnd}(0, [50, 50]) \tag{39}$$

$$P_0^+ = \begin{bmatrix} 50^2 & 0 \\ 0 & 50^2 \end{bmatrix} \tag{40}$$

The above equation means the error of the initial guess for the target state is randomly sampled from a Gaussian distribution with a standard deviation of $[50, 50]$.

The time history of RMSE of the navigation is shown in **Figure 9**. One can observe the RMSE converges relatively slower than other examples. Because the TRN estimates 2D position by using the height measurements, it often lacks information on the vehicle state. Moreover, note that the extended Kalman filter linearizes the terrain model and deals with the slope that is effective locally. If the gradient of the terrain is zero, the measurement matrix H has zero-diagonal terms that has zero effect on the state correction. In this case, the measurement is called ambiguous [12] and this ambiguous measurement often causes filter degradation and divergence even in nonlinear filtering techniques. With highly nonlinear terrain models, TRN systems have recently been constructed with other nonlinear filtering methods such as point-mass filters and particle filters, rather than extended Kalman filters.

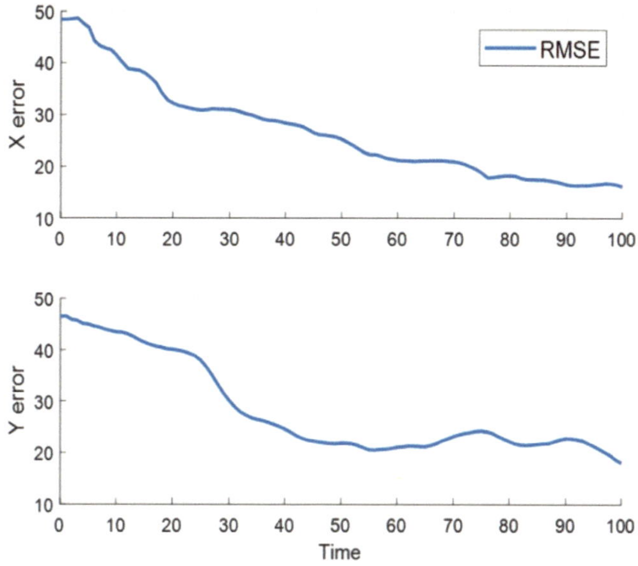

Figure 9.
Time history of RMSE.

Source code of MATLAB implementation for this example can be found in [5]. It is recommended for the readers to change the parameters and aircraft trajectory by yourself and see what happens.

4. Conclusion

In this chapter, we introduced the Kalman filter and extended Kalman filter algorithms. INS/GNSS navigation, target tracking, and terrain-referenced navigation were provided as examples for reader's better understanding of practical usage of the Kalman filters. This chapter will become a prerequisite for other contents in the book for those who do not have a strong background in estimation theory.

Author details

Youngjoo Kim* and Hyochoong Bang
Korea Advanced Institute of Science and Technology, Daejeon, South Korea

*Address all correspondence to: yjkim@ascl.kaist.ac.kr

References

[1] Simon D. Optimal State Estimation: Kalman, H Infinity, and Nonlinear Approaches. Oxford: John Wiley & Sons; 2006

[2] Li XR, Jilkov VP. Survey of maneuvering target tracking. Part I. Dynamic models. IEEE Transactions on Aerospace and Electronic Systems. 2003;**39**(4):1333-1364

[3] Rajamani MR, Rawlings JB. Estimation of the disturbance structure from data using semidefinite programming and optimal weighting. Automatica. 2009;**45**(1):142-148

[4] Matisko P, Havlena V. Noise covariance estimation for Kalman filter tuning using Bayesian approach and Monte Carlo. International Journal of Adaptive Control and Signal Processing. 2013;**27**(11):957-973

[5] Introduction to Kalman Filter and Its Applications. 2018. Available from: https://uk.mathworks.com/matlabcentral/fileexchange/68262-introduction-to-kalman-filter-and-its-applications

[6] Kim Y, Jung W, Bang H. Real-time path planning to dispatch a mobile sensor into an operational area. Information Fusion. 2019;**45**:27-37

[7] Kim Y, Bang H. Vision-based navigation for unmanned aircraft using ground feature points and terrain elevation data. Proceedings of the Institution of Mechanical Engineers, Part G: Journal of Aerospace Engineering. 2018;**232**(7):1334-1346

[8] Vadlamani AK, de Haag MU. Dual airborne laser scanners aided inertial for improved autonomous navigation. IEEE Transactions on Aerospace and Electronic Systems. 2009;**45**(4):1483-1498

[9] Kim Y, Park J, Bang H. Terrain referenced navigation using an interferometric radar altimeter, NAVIGATION. Journal of the Institute of Navigation. 2018;**65**(2):157-167

[10] Rogers RM. Applied mathematics in integrated navigation systems. American Institute of Aeronautics and Astronautics. 2007

[11] Interpolation. Available from: https://en.wikipedia.org/w/index.php?title=Interpolation&oldid=765887238

[12] Kim Y, Hong K, Bang H. Utilizing out-of-sequence measurement for ambiguous update in particle filtering. IEEE Transactions on Aerospace and Electronic Systems. 2018;**54**(1):493-501

Section 2

Kalman Filter Implementations

Chapter 3

Tuning of the Kalman Filter Using Constant Gains

Mudambi R. Ananthasayanam

Abstract

For designing an optimal Kalman filter, it is necessary to specify the statistics, namely the initial state, its covariance and the process and measurement noise covariances. These can be chosen by minimising some suitable cost function **J**. This has been very difficult till recently when a near optimal Recurrence Reference Recipe (**RRR**) was proposed without any optimisation but only filtering. In many filter applications after the initial transients, the gain matrix **K** tends to a constant during the steady state, which points to design the filter based on constant gains alone. Such a constant gain Kalman filter (**CGKF**) can be designed by minimising any suitable cost function. Since there are no covariances in **CGKF,** only the state equations need to be propagated and updated at a measurement, thus enormously reducing the computational load. Though **CGKF** results may not be too close to those of **RRR,** they are acceptable. It accepts extremely simple models and the gains are robust in handling similar scenarios. In this chapter, we provide examples of applying the **CGKF** by ancient Indian astronomers, parameter estimation of spring, mass and damper system, airplane real flight test data, ballistic rocket, re-entry of space object and the evolution of space debris.

Keywords: adaptive EKF, reference recursive recipe, maximum likelihood, Cramer Rao bound, constant gain Kalman filter

1. Introduction to Kalman filter

The simplest formulation of a Kalman filter [1] is when the state and measurement equations are both linear. However, Kalman filter has found its greatest application for non-linear systems. A typical continuous state with discrete measurements in time forming a non-linear filtering problem can be written as

$$\mathbf{x}(k) = \mathbf{f}(\mathbf{x}(k-1), \boldsymbol{\Theta}, \mathbf{u}(k-1)) + \mathbf{w}(k), \tag{1}$$

$$Z(k) = \mathbf{h}(\mathbf{x}(k, \boldsymbol{\Theta})) + \mathbf{v}(k), k = 1, 2, 3, \ldots, \mathbf{N} \tag{2}$$

where '**x**' and 'Z' are, respectively, the state and measurement equations of size (n × 1) and (m × 1); **u** is the control input and **Θ** the parameter vector of size (p × 1) and '**f**' and '**h**' are non-linear functions. The process '**w**' and measurement '**v**' noises are respectively of size (n × 1) and (m × 1). These are assumed to be zero mean with covariances **Q** and **R** and their sequences are uncorrelated with each other. The states may not be in general observable but the measurements should be related to the states. In many applications for linear systems, if the unknown

 IntechOpen

parameters $\mathbf{\Theta}$ are treated as additional states, then the linear system of equations becomes non-linear. In such cases, the extended Kalman filter (**EKF**) formulation can be written as

$$\begin{bmatrix} \mathbf{x}(k) \\ \mathbf{\Theta}(k) \end{bmatrix} = \begin{bmatrix} \mathbf{f}(\mathbf{x}(k-1), \ \mathbf{\Theta}(k-1), \mathbf{u}(k-1)) \\ \mathbf{\Theta}(k-1) \end{bmatrix} + \begin{bmatrix} \mathbf{w}(k) \\ 0 \end{bmatrix} \tag{3}$$

or equivalently

$$\mathbf{X}(k) = \mathbf{f}(\mathbf{X}(k-1)) + \mathbf{w}(k) \tag{4}$$

$$\mathbf{Z}(k) = \mathbf{h}(\mathbf{X}(k)) + \mathbf{v}(k), \quad k = 1, 2, \ldots, \mathbf{N} \tag{5}$$

where '$\mathbf{X}$' is the augmented state of size $((n+p) \times 1)$. The control symbol '$\mathbf{u}$' is not shown for brevity. The formal solution for the above filtering problem can be summarised following Brown and Hwang [2] as

$$\text{Initial state estimate } \mathbf{X}(0|0) = \mathbf{X0} = \mathbf{E}\,[\mathbf{X}(t0)], \tag{6}$$

$$\text{Initial state covariance matrix } \mathbf{P}(0|0) = \mathbf{P0} = \mathbf{E}\left[(\mathbf{X0}\text{–}\mathbf{X}(t0))(\mathbf{X0}\text{–}\mathbf{X}(t0))^{T}\right] \tag{7}$$

$$\text{Prediction step: } \mathbf{X}(k|k-1) = \mathbf{f}(\mathbf{X}(k-1|k-1)), \tag{8}$$

$$\mathbf{P}(k|k-1) = \mathbf{F}(k-1)\mathbf{P}(k-1|k-1)\mathbf{F}(k-1)^{T} + \mathbf{Q}(k) \tag{9}$$

We assume that $\mathbf{X}(k|k-1)$ and $\mathbf{P}(k|k-1)$ denote the estimates of the state and its covariance matrix, respectively, at time index k, based on all information available up to and including time index k–1. Then, we seek to update the state value from $\mathbf{X}\,(k|k-1)$ to $\mathbf{X}\,(k|k)$ using the measurement $\mathbf{Z}(k)$ with uncertainty denoted by $\mathbf{R}(k)$ based on the value of $\mathbf{K}(k)$ called the Kalman gain such that the updated covariance $\mathbf{P}(k|k)$ having the individual terms along its major diagonal is a minimum, leading to

$$\text{Update step: } \mathbf{K}(k) = \mathbf{P}(k|k-1)\ \mathbf{H}(k)^{T}\left[\mathbf{H}(k)\ \mathbf{P}(k|k-1)\ \mathbf{H}(k)^{T} + \mathbf{R}(k)\right]^{-1} \tag{10}$$

$$\mathbf{X}(k|k) = \mathbf{X}(k|k-1) + \mathbf{K}(k)[\mathbf{Z}(k)\text{–}\mathbf{h}(\mathbf{X}(k|k-1))] = \mathbf{X}(k|k-1) + \mathbf{K}(k)\boldsymbol{\nu}(k) \tag{11}$$

$$\mathbf{P}(k|k) = [\mathbf{I} - \mathbf{K}(k)\mathbf{H}(k)]\mathbf{P}(k|k-1) \tag{12}$$

with $\mathbf{P}$ denoting uncertainty, $\mathbf{F}(k-1)$ is the state Jacobian matrix $(\partial\mathbf{f}/\partial\mathbf{X})$ evaluated at $\mathbf{X} = \mathbf{X}(k-1|k-1)$. $\mathbf{X}(k|k-1)$ denotes the estimate at t(k) based on the process dynamics between t(k–1) and t(k) but before using the measurement information. The measurement Jacobian $\mathbf{H}(k) = (\partial\mathbf{h}/\partial\mathbf{X})$ is evaluated at $\mathbf{X} = \mathbf{X}(k)$. The difference between the actual measurement and the predicted model output

$$\boldsymbol{\nu}(\mathbf{k}) = [\mathbf{Z}(k)\text{–}\mathbf{h}(\mathbf{X}(k|k-1))] \tag{13}$$

is called the innovation. The importance of the innovation following white Gaussian for filter performance was brought out by Kailath [3]. When the innovation is white, it means all the information has been extracted from the data and no further information is left out, thus both the models and the algorithm have done their best job.

There are thus five basic filter operations, namely: (i) the state propagation, (ii) the covariance propagation, (iii) Kalman gain evaluation, (iv) the state update and (v) the covariance update. The first and fourth refer to sample values and the second, third and fifth refer to the population characteristics. At any given time point, the statistical combination of the two estimates, one from state and the other from measurement equation, are formal if only the covariances denoting their uncertainties are available. Thus the states and the covariances at all times can be estimated if the initial **X0** and **P0** as well as **Q(k)** and **R(k)** are specified over time, but this is not easy. These have to be specified over a time span in order to match and minimise a cost function based on the innovation, or any other in some best possible sense. A well-known criterion is the method of maximum likelihood estimation (**MMLE**). When $\mathbf{Q} \equiv 0$, the Kalman gain matrix is zero and the technique is called as the output error method (**MMLE-OEM**). When $\mathbf{Q} > 0$, the method is called as filter error method [4, 5]. For optimal design of the Kalman filter, the innovation follows a white Gaussian distribution which is operationally equivalent to minimising the cost function

$$\mathbf{J} = (\mathbf{1/N})\Sigma\, \boldsymbol{\nu}(\mathbf{k}) \left[\mathbf{H}(\mathrm{k})\mathbf{P}(\mathrm{k}|\mathrm{k}-1)\mathbf{H}(\mathbf{k})^{\mathrm{T}} + \mathbf{R}(\mathrm{k})\right]^{-1} \boldsymbol{\nu}(\mathbf{k})^{\mathrm{T}} \tag{14}$$

$$= (\mathbf{1/N})\Sigma\, \boldsymbol{\nu}(\mathbf{k})\ [\mathcal{R}]^{-1}\boldsymbol{\nu}(\mathbf{k})^{\mathrm{T}}\ \mathbf{or} \tag{15}$$

$$= \mathbf{J}(\mathbf{X0}, \mathbf{P0}, \mathbf{Q}, \mathbf{R}, \boldsymbol{\Theta})\ \text{or} \tag{16}$$

$$= \mathbf{J}\ (\mathbf{X0}, \boldsymbol{\Theta}, \mathbf{K}(\text{traded for}, \mathbf{P0}, \mathbf{Q}, \text{and}, \mathbf{R})) \tag{17}$$

based on summation over all the **N** measurements. Thus, the filter has to be tuned or in other words should solve for either the statistics **X0, Θ, P0, Q** and **R,** in Eq. (16), or for **X0, Θ** and **K** in Eq. (17). Of course, there have been many number of cost functions used in the literature, the only constraint being all should lead to reasonable answers that are acceptable. The $\mathbf{Q} \equiv 0$ case leads to an optimisation of the cost function. If $\mathbf{Q} > 0$, then the filter approach becomes compulsive and generally the cost function is forgotten and mostly the filter statistics are tuned manually to obtain the results.

One can see straightaway that the structure of the above cost function **J** becomes different due to the change of variables (different combination of the statistics can lead to the same gain!); and hence whatever the results are generated, they will be different but have to be within reasonable limits. In the **RRR** studies [6–9], many typical cost functions have been stated to bring home the above point. One can be around the true answer but not at the answer which is not known due to the occurrence of the random unknown sequence of the noise distribution in the data. Hence, estimation theory being an inverse problem, the results are subjective and not objective as many claim. In fact, the whole of statistics is subjective from the beginning to the end and thus the results generated can be stretched to any limit but have to be meaningful, acceptable and useful for further use. As is well known, inverse problems do not have unique answers, more so with randomness being introduced. Unless the above sequence of noise distribution can be worked out correctly, there is no way to get the true answers. Thus, the statistical percolation effect affects all the unknowns in any estimation theory. This should be kept in mind to understand any result based on filter statistics or filter gains in Kalman filtering.

1.1 The competence and beauty of the Kalman filter

The earliest Kalman filter formulation by Kalman [1] dealt with state estimation. However, it has grown at present to handle myriad other scenarios such as state and parameter estimation, data fusion and many more. The Kalman filter can ably estimate or account for time-invariant or time-varying (i) unknown, (ii) inaccurately known or (iii) even unmodellable structure of the state and measurement model equations and the parameters in them as also (iv) the deterministic or random inputs and by accounting for them suitably as process and measurement noises. It can compensate even for computational errors during the entire filter operation.

Further, the state and covariance updates at a measurement depend only on the covariances of the state and the measurements and not their probability distribution (!). Hence, after assimilating the measurement information, the update is subtly reset to follow a Gaussian distribution. Thus, the use of only the estimate and covariance all over the filter tacitly implies (one can however improve the numerical values of the estimate and covariance in non-linear problems) the state and measurement variables are all distributed or approximated as quasi-Gaussian. Hence, with all such subjective features, the final result can only be an answer rather than a true or unique answer. All the above have to be checked for the consistency of the whole process of modelling, convergence of the numerical algorithm and other consistency checks among the variables occurring in the filter as discussed in [6, 10–12].

1.2 Use of filter statistics in designing the Kalman filter

Assuming that the measurements are available at **N** discrete time instants, the normalised innovation cost function **J** fundamental to the Kalman filter as suggested by Sorenson [13] is defined as

$$\mathbf{J} = (\mathbf{1/N})\Sigma\, \boldsymbol{\nu}(\mathbf{k})\ \ [\mathcal{R}]^{-1}\boldsymbol{\nu}(\mathbf{k})^{\mathrm{T}} \tag{18}$$

where $\mathcal{R}$ is the covariance matrix of the innovation $\left[\mathbf{H}(\mathrm{k})\mathbf{P}(\mathrm{k}|\mathrm{k}-1)\mathbf{H}(\mathbf{k})^{\mathrm{T}} + \mathbf{R}(\mathrm{k})\right]$. Here, $\mathcal{R}$ which is a function of **P0**, **Q** and **R** varies with time. The estimation of the system parameters **X0, Θ, P0, Q** and **R** is called filter design or filter tuning as mentioned earlier. Though there are many techniques for adaptively tuning the filter statistics [14], the recent **RRR** [6–9] or the heuristic approach of Myers and Tapley [15] for **Q**, and **R**, and of Gemson [16] and Gemson and Ananthasayanam [17] for **P0** are perhaps the simplest ones.

1.3 Use of filter gains and design of constant gain Kalman filter (CGKF)

In the constant Kalman gain formulation (in discrete form), the update step

$$\mathbf{K}(\mathrm{k}) = \mathbf{P}(\mathrm{k}|\mathrm{k}-1)\ \mathbf{H}(\mathrm{k})^{\mathrm{T}}\left[\mathbf{H}(\mathrm{k})\ \mathbf{P}(\mathrm{k}|\mathrm{k}-1)\ \mathbf{H}(\mathrm{k})^{\mathrm{T}} + \mathbf{R}(\mathrm{k})\right]^{-1} \tag{19}$$

$$\mathbf{X}(\mathrm{k}|\mathrm{k}) = \mathbf{X}(\mathrm{k}|\mathrm{k}-1) + \mathbf{K}(\mathrm{k})[\mathbf{Z}(\mathrm{k})\text{–}\mathbf{h}(\mathbf{X}(\mathrm{k}|\mathrm{k}-1))] = \mathbf{X}(\mathrm{k}|\mathrm{k}-1) + \mathbf{K}(\mathrm{k})\boldsymbol{\nu}_{\mathbf{k}} \tag{20}$$

$$\mathbf{P}(\mathrm{k}|\mathrm{k}) = [\mathbf{I} - \mathbf{K}(\mathrm{k})\mathbf{H}(\mathrm{k})]\mathbf{P}(\mathrm{k}|\mathrm{k}-1) \tag{21}$$

gets simplified to determine only the constant gain matrix **K**(k) by subsuming **P0, Q** and **R**. Hence, there are no covariance equations for propagation at all, thus enormously reducing the numerical effort and time. The constant filter gain approach is less explored than the filter statistics approach. Many attempts have been made by Wilson [18], Cook and Dawson [19], Grimble et al. [20], Kobayashi [21] and Liu et al. [22]; but these are not simple, except the modified gain extended Kalman filter (**MGEF**) proposed by Song and Speyer [23]. Gelb [24] and Sugiyama [25] consider the **CGKF** approach but their method of tuning the desired filter gain parameters is manual. The present rational procedure is based on a suitable normalised innovation cost function as in space debris [26–29] and many other illustrative examples to follow.

When a regular Kalman filter using the filter statistics operates on the data in general, it turns out that after the initial transients the Kalman gain matrix tends to a constant value. Such a feature has been noticed in the tracking of ballistic rockets by Sarkar [30], evolution and expansion of the space debris scenario and prediction of re-entry objects [27–29]; for parameter estimation of dynamic systems by Viswanath [31]; in rendezvous and docking studies [32, 33] and total electron content in the ionosphere [34, 35] and in integration of **GPS** and **INS** [36, 37], target tracking in wireless sensor networks by Yadav et al. [38] and many more. Due to limited space, only the first three will be discussed in this chapter. This observation provides a possible approach in which instead of tuning the usual Kalman filter statistics for **X0, P0, Q** and **R,** in general, a smaller number of Kalman gain elements can be worked out. This constant gain matrix **K** can be obtained by making the above normalised innovation cost function equal to the number of measurements by assuming the above $\mathcal{R}$ in Eq. (18) to be a constant. Then, the $\mathcal{R}$ can be estimated as if it is the estimation of pure noise only as is the case of **MMLE-OEM** [4, 5]. There could be some differences in the gain values obtained from the adaptively or manually tuned **P0, Q** and **R** and the constant gain approach due to the relative periods of transients and the steady-state conditions. Though the results may not be as close to the optimum, the estimates are generally acceptable. The present examples mostly utilise the genetic algorithm [39, 40] to minimise the cost function **J** and obtain optimum **K.** However, before applying the constant Kalman gain approach, it is desirable to carry out extensive studies using any adequate adaptive filtering technique such as **RRR.** A comparison of the results from the adaptive technique and the constant Kalman gain approach provides confidence in the latter approach. The following sections provide example applications of designing constant gain Kalman filters.

2. Ancient Indian astronomers implicitly using the constant Kalman gain approach

Ancient Indian astronomers needed to calculate the position of celestial objects like Sun, Moon and other planets for timing the Vedic rituals. But their predicted positions changed over many centuries due to unmodelled or unmodellable causes. The philosophy of 'change, capture and correct' is the one that is followed in the Kalman filter. The ancient Indian astronomers had understood the above philosophy. They used the above concept to update the parameters for predicting the position of celestial objects based on measurements carried out at various time intervals which can be stated as.

$$\begin{aligned}&\text{Updated parameter} = \text{Earlier parameter} + (\text{Some quantity})\times\\&(\text{Measured} - \text{Predicted})\ \text{Position of the celestial object}\end{aligned} \tag{22}$$

They could not have done it in any other way to update the earlier parameters called 'cannons'. The 'some quantity' as we will see later on is the Kalman gain. There were no frills and fashion of distributions and the spread to infer uncertainties after combining statistically one estimate in certain units with another estimate in another unit but related to the former. The measured longitude of the celestial object is different from the state that is updated, which is the number of revolutions in a yuga just as state and measurements are in general different in many Kalman filter applications!

Billard [41, 42] had stated that if the elements of Aryabhata are now wrong, they must have been accurate when he was living. Then, newer astronomical elements can be established based on the earlier astronomical elements and the new observations of the present time. Billard [41, 42] provides many cannons starting from around AD 500 by Aryabhata to AD 1600 based on later measurements carried out (over many years or even decades!) to make the predicted position of the objects consistent with new observations. One such canon around AD 898 shows a very high accuracy valid over a larger number of centuries. Sarma [43] quotes such revisions over a period of time. Nilakantha (around AD 1443) had stated that the eclipses cited in Siddhanthas as well as those currently observable can be studied and future eclipses can be predicted (extrapolation!). Also, for the eclipses occurring at other longitudes and latitudes, the predictions can be perfected (data fusion!). Based on these, the past eclipses of one's own place can be refined equivalent to 'smoothing'! It is strongly urged that research is undertaken on Billard's work available in French.

3. Typical parameter estimation studies

In order to illustrate the ability of **CGKF**, we consider the parameter estimation of a spring, mass and damper (**SMD**) system with a weak non-linear spring constant and also a real flight test data of an airplane.

3.1 Analysis of spring, mass and damper (SMD) system

The **SMD** system with weak non-linear spring constant in continuous time (t) is governed by the equations

$$\dot{x_1}(t) = x_2\,(t) \tag{23}$$

$$\dot{x_2}(t) = -\Theta_1 x_1(t) - \Theta_2 x_2(t) - \Theta_3 x_1^3\,(t) \tag{24}$$

where x_1 and x_2 are the displacement and velocity states. The 'dot' represents differentiation with respect to time (t). The unknown parameter vector $\mathbf{\Theta} = [\Theta_1, \Theta_2, \Theta_3]^T$ has the true value $\mathbf{\Theta_{true}} = \mathbf{[4, 0.4, 0.6]}$. Θ_3 being a weak parameter, it does not affect the system dynamics much and hence its estimation also has more uncertainty. The complete state vector $\mathbf{X} = [x_1, x_2, \Theta_1, \Theta_2, \Theta_3]^T$ of size $[(n + p) \times 1]$ which in this case is (5×1). The measurement equation is given by.

$$\mathbf{Z}(\mathrm{k}) = \mathbf{H}\,\mathbf{X}(\mathrm{k}) \tag{25}$$

where $\mathbf{H} = \begin{bmatrix} 1 & 0 & 0 & 0 & 0 \\ 0 & 1 & 0 & 0 & 0 \end{bmatrix}$ is the measurement matrix of size $(m \times (n + p))$ where $m = n = 2$ and $p = 3$.

At a measurement with the additional terms to assimilate the measurement data, the above equations become

$$\dot{x_1}(t) = x_2\,(t) + K_{11}(Z_1 - x_1) + K_{12}(Z_2 - x_2) \tag{26}$$

$$\dot{x_2}(t) = -\Theta_1 x_1(t) - \Theta_2 x_2(t) - \Theta_3 x_1^3(t) + K_{21}(Z_1 - x_1) + K_{22}(Z_2 - x_2) \tag{27}$$

where K_{11}, K_{12}, K_{21} and K_{22} are the elements of the constant Kalman gain matrix **K**. These along with the parameter vector $\mathbf{\Theta}$ have to be estimated by minimising the earlier mentioned innovation cost function **J**. A total of $\mathbf{N} = 100$ simulated measurement data are generated with initial state conditions 1 and 0, respectively, in steps of dt = 0.1 s between time 0 and 10 s.

3.2 Remarks on the SMD parameter estimation

The **CGKF** were based on 25 Newton-Raphson iterations and **RRR** results were generated based on 100 iterations for each data set (for obtaining generally four-digit accuracy though not necessary) and are compared in **Table 1** below. The parameter values are to be read as for $[\boldsymbol{\Theta}_1, \boldsymbol{\Theta}_2, \boldsymbol{\Theta}_3]$. For $\mathbf{Q} \equiv 0$ and $\mathbf{Q} > 0$ cases, the mean and standard deviation of the parameter estimates from **CGKF** and **RRR** are by and large close. In fact, the **CGKF** estimates are generally within about $\mathbf{1\sigma}$ of the CRB values given by **RRR.** In the **RRR** with constant **P0**, **Q** and **R,** the filter is able to follow the system fairly well due to the time-varying gains providing near optimal solution. But in the **CGKF** approach, since the gains are constant, the filter is unable to follow the system model as well as by **RRR**. Thus, **CGKF** follows a slightly different dynamical model than **RRR** and hence their results are somewhat different.

The gains are to be read as first column first and the second column next. For **CGKF,** there are only four gains associated with the two states and two measurements. But for **RRR,** there are ten gains associated with five states and two measurements. For the case of $\mathbf{Q} \equiv 0$, all the gains should have been ideally zero but are around zero here due to the statistical percolation effect of the unforgiving noises, be it process and/or measurement. This affects not just one parameter or state but every other quantity, so the gains or any estimated quantity in the numerical algorithm can also never take their true values except perhaps with an appropriate algorithm that can capture the true values with increasing amount of data. For the $\mathbf{Q} > 0$ case, the major gains marked in bold are somewhat similar.

SMD SYSTEM: For CGKF, the standard deviation (STDV) is based on parameter estimates and for RRR, the Cramer-Rao Bound (CRB ~ STDV) is based on filter covariance averaged over 100 simulations		
Results for the three parameters		
Case	**Mean**	**STDV**
CGKF Q ≡ 0	3.9982 0.3994 0.5948	0.0377 0.0112 0.0954
RRR Q ≡ 0	4.0028 0.4000 0.5921	0.0242 0.0055 0.0677
CGKF Q > 0	4.0467 0.4115 0.5734	0.2218 0.0682 0.4862
RRR Q > 0	3.9770 0.4085 0.6456	0.2337 0.0714 0.4047
Results for the gain		
Case	**Mean**	**STDV**
CGKF Q ≡ 0	−0.0655 0.0002 0.0027 -0.0758	0.0410 0.0286 0.1129 0.0529
RRR Q ≡ 0	0.0184 0.0077 −0.0955 −0.0038 0.2001 0.0019 0.0096 −0.0169 0.0055 0.0457	0.0020 0.0014 0.0102 0.0006 0.0216 0.0002 0.0009 0.0018 0.0006 0.0045
CGKF Q > 0	**0.6249** −0.0038 −0.0017 **0.4401**	0.1199 0.0460 0.2033 0.1246
RRR Q > 0	**0.6347** −0.0097 −0.0424 0.0111 0.0711 −0.0035 **0.5409** −0.0796 0.0330 0.1417	0.0737 0.0107 0.0487 0.0087 0.0702 0.0035 0.0886 0.1506 0.0218 0.2206

Table 1.
Comparison of simulated SMD data results of CGKF with RRR.

3.3 Analysis of real airplane flight test data

This real data set discussed earlier in [6, 8, 9] is obtained along with airplane, flight test data and notations from [44]. Briefly, to explain the scenario, there is a peculiar manoeuvre when the aircraft (T 37 B) is rolling through a full rotation using the aileron, and then the elevator angle (δ_e in deg) is imparted. The coupling between the longitudinal and lateral motion is replaced by their measured values, namely the roll angle (φ_m), sideslip (β_m), velocity (V_m), roll rate (p_m), yaw rate (r_m) and the angle of attack (α_m). The state equations (n = 3) for the angle of attack (α), pitch rate (q) and the pitch angle (θ), respectively, are

$$\begin{aligned}\dot{\alpha} = &-\frac{\bar{q}\,S}{mV_m\,Cos\,(\beta_m)}\left(C_{L_\alpha}\,\alpha + C_{L_{\delta_e}}\delta_e + C_{L_0}\right)\\ &+q+\frac{g}{V_m\,Cos\,(\beta_m)}(\cos(\phi_m)(\cos(\alpha_m)\cos(\theta)+\sin(\alpha_m)\,\sin(\theta))\\ &-\tan(\beta_m)(p_m\cos(\alpha_m)+r_m\,\sin\alpha_m))\end{aligned} \tag{28}$$

$$\dot{q} = \frac{\bar{q}\,S\,\bar{c}}{I_{yy}}\left(C_{m_\alpha}\alpha + C_{m_q}\frac{\bar{c}}{2V}q + C_{m\dot{\alpha}}\frac{\bar{c}}{2V}\dot{\alpha} + C_{m_{\delta_e}}\delta_e + C_{m0}\right) + \frac{I_{zz}-I_{xx}}{I_{yy}}r_m p_m \tag{29}$$

$$\dot{\theta} = q\cos(\phi_m) - r_m\sin(\phi_m) + \theta_0 \tag{30}$$

The measurement equations (m = 4) for the angle of attack, pitch rate, pitch and normal acceleration are given by

$$\alpha_m = K_\alpha\,\alpha - K_\alpha x_\alpha\frac{q}{V}\;; \tag{31}$$

$$q_m = q\;; \tag{32}$$

$$\theta_m = \theta \tag{33}$$

$$a_{n_m} = \frac{\bar{q}\,S}{mg}\left(C_{N_\alpha}\alpha + C_{N_{\delta_e}}\delta_e + C_{N_0}\right) + \frac{x_{a_n}}{g}\dot{q} \tag{34}$$

The unknown parameters (p = 10) are $\left(C_{L_\alpha}, C_{L_{\delta_e}}, C_{L_0}, C_{m_\alpha}, C_{m_q}, C_{m\dot{\alpha}}, C_{m_{\delta_e}}, C_{m_0}, \theta_0, C_{N_0}\right)^T$ with the approximation $C_{N_\alpha} = C_{L_\alpha}$ and $C_{N_{\delta_e}} = C_{L_{\delta_e}}$. The suffix δ_e denotes control derivatives, and suffix zero refers to biases and all others are aerodynamic derivatives. The initial states are taken as the initial measurements and the initial parameter values are taken as $(4, 0.15, 0.2, -0.5, -11.5, -5, -1.38, -0.06, -0.01, 0.2)^T$. At a measurement similar to the **SMD** system, there is an additional term $\mathbf{K}\boldsymbol{\nu}(\mathbf{k})$ which is the product of the gain matrix multiplying the innovation.

3.4 Remarks on the real flight test data results

Table 2 below compares the parameter estimates and their **CRB**s (in parenthesis) from the **RRR** [6, 8, 9], Gemson [16], (derived from the filter covariance) and **CGKF** (based on cost function) approaches. The parameter estimates from the first two are comparable except for the parameters $C_{L_{\delta_e}}$ and C_{m_q} which strongly affect the airplane dynamics. However, all the parameter estimates from **RRR,** Gemson and **CGKF** are quite comparable. The **CGKF** estimates are within about **1σ** of the **RRR** values as in the previous **SMD** case. The **STDV** from the **CGKF** (corresponding to **CRB)** is somewhat different from the other approaches since it follows a slightly different dynamical model than **RRR** or Gemson as in the **SMD** case.

Θ	*RRR*	Gemson	CGKF
C_{N_0}	0.2538 (0.0014)	0.2503 (0.0014)	0.2512 (0.0006)
C_{L_0}	0.2409 (0.0021)	0.2529 (0.0018)	0.2443 (0.0019)
C_{L_α}	4.9235 (0.0164)	4.9028 (0.0168)	4.8035 (0.2199)
$C_{L_{\delta_e}}$	0.1554 (0.0271)	0.0879 (0.0267)	0.1653 (0.0993)
C_{m_0}	−0.0425 (0.0009)	−0.0507 (0.0024)	−0.0459 (0.0001)
C_{m_α}	−0.5293 (0.0079)	−0.6174 (0.0211)	−0.4986 (0.0345)
C_{m_q}	−11.8596 (0.2402)	−18.8339 (.8379)	−9.3528 (2.1234)
$C_{m\dot{\alpha}}$	−6.8959 (0.4891)	−7.1290 (1.544)	−6.6730 (4.6084)
$C_{m_{\delta_e}}$	−0.9731 (0.0177)	−1.1841 (0.471)	−1.0063 (0.0019)
θ_0	0.0003 (0.0021)	−0.0037 (0.001)	0.0020 (0.0003)

Table 2.
Comparison of real flight test data results (Θ, $\sigma(\Theta)$).

4. Introduction to flight data analysis of a ballistic rocket (BR)

During the development of any **BR,** it is necessary to carry out many flight trials and compare the flight performance with that based on pre-flight estimates. For a **BR**, an accurate estimation of drag coefficient is very important due to its direct impact on the system performance as it plays a very critical role in generating the firing tables. One also uses wind tunnel tests or computational fluid dynamic codes to obtain the aerodynamic characteristics. But there exist generally unavoidable errors due to wind tunnel wall interference and the limitation of wind tunnel Reynolds number. Hence, the assessment of the aerodynamic coefficient from the full-scale flight test of vehicles is an important area of activity and research. Such an analysis would help the **BR** as follows.

1. If it fails en route, a real-time state estimation helps to obtain the expected impact location from range safety viewpoint.

2. A compatibility check of measured data reduces bias and scale factor effects in the measurements. The measurement noise covariances given in the manufacturer's catalogues being notional, such values can also be estimated.

3. In its external ballistics, the variation of aerodynamic drag coefficient with respect to Mach number is very important.

4. Comparison of pre-flight with flight test estimated drag coefficient helps to improve and modify the former.

4.1 State estimation of a ballistic rocket (BR)

It is possible to formulate the Kalman Filter (**KF**) to simultaneously estimate both the state and parameter or carry out the same sequentially. In the state estimation step, the bias, scale and the random errors are estimated, called compatibility check, and thus relatively clean data are available for parameter estimation. The **BR**s are generally tracked by ground based radar, which provides range, azimuth and elevation measurements. Sarkar explains in [30] the extended Kalman filter

[24] together with a smoother for handling the effect of both the process and measurement noise contained in the measured flight test data. Later, it is used to estimate the aerodynamic drag coefficient (which is a parameter estimation problem) using the **MMLE-OEM** approach. We discuss here only his trajectory estimation by using **CGKF** and the reader can refer to [30] for drag estimation.

In order to track the trajectory of a **BR,** one can use either the dynamical or the kinematical equations. The former needs many inputs such as the forces and moments, propulsion and the control which may not be available and more so if the **BR** belongs to an adversary. Broadly, the three approaches all utilising the kinematic state equations for trajectory estimation with increasing accuracy are

1. The 'generic' ones called α, αβ or αβγ types of filters as found in Blair [45] and Bar-Shalom and Li [46].

2. The 'similar' ones like the **CGKF** approach which can handle similar situations.

3. The 'specific' one for a given scenario like the adaptive extended Kalman filter (**AEKF**) such as by Gemson [16] or the ones like the adaptive limited memory filter (**ALMF**) as in [15].

The **AEKF/ALMF** deals with a specific scenario and adaptively obtains **Q** and **R** by minimising the cost function **J** in Eq. (16) and the steady-state gain **K** follows. The second **CGKF** handles the same specific scenario by minimising the cost function **J** in Eq. (17) and obtains the gain **K** directly**.** Due to the transformed unknown variables, the results for **K** will be somewhat different but close to **AEKF**. The gain being more robust, **CGKF** can handle similar situations. In order to account for model deficiencies or uncertainties in real cases, these constant gains can be increased from the ones based on simulated studies. The αβγ types of filters define a manoeuvre index called λ (based on a subjective choice of **Q** , and **R,** and the time between measurements) which leads to the various gains. Thus, λ being chosen subjectively, the model accountability is generic. Such filters also do not consider any cost function, whereas the second and third are two routes to tune the Kalman filter by minimising **J,** the normalised innovation sequence (**NIS**) cost function. The only way to improve the performance of αβγ types of filters is to tune the λ manually as is shown later.

The filter world kinematic model equations could consist of displacement, velocity, acceleration, jerk, slack and so on driven by inputs at the highest state derivative variables as chosen by the analyst. The inputs could be random white noise or even correlated noise. If the input is a random white noise, then the corresponding state variable and lower ones become Gauss-Markov (**GM**) processes of increasingly higher order.

One cannot drive the displacement by white noise since no real-world system can be instantaneously displaced due to its finite mass and moment of inertia. It is best to introduce the input at higher levels as a white or correlated Gaussian noise as in Mehrotra and Mahapatra [47], or Singer [48]. Usually, the input being a white noise acceleration, its integration provides velocity and the further integration leads to displacement. Hence, the displacement would become a third-order **GM** process. If the input is at the velocity level, then the displacement becomes second-order Gauss-Markov process. The input at the jerk or the slack would increase the order of the filter equations. Hence, the analyst has to choose the input acceleration at a level to provide a reasonable balance between the model order and the anticipated dynamic rate of change of the object.

4.2 Comparison of second and third order Gauss Markov system model in CGKF

Here, we consider the nine state variables as ($R, \dot{R}, \ddot{R}, A, \dot{A}, \ddot{A}, E, \dot{E}, \ddot{E}$) and the three measurements as (R, A, E), both in polar coordinates, and the specific to real-time application in the so called **PPR** [30] frame. The estimation error of the state variables' position and velocity based on the second and third order model shows it is more in the former than in the latter. This is due to the simple fact that in the second order model, the accelerations are not accounted for properly during the transition from boost phase to power off coast, when there is a rapid change in **BR** acceleration level, which is not taken into account in the second-order model unlike in the third order model [30].

4.3 Filter tuning using CGKF and adaptive estimation of (P0, Q, R)

We consider both the above **ALMF** and the simpler **CGKF** for real-time processing to gain confidence in the results. In the former, the choice of window length is important to reach the **NIS** equal to the number of measurements for filter tuning. The adaptive filter tuning of the statistics **P0, Q** and **R** has been carried out by varying the window length **L** to track the **NIS** Cost towards 3 as shown in **Figure 1**. The next **Figure 2** shows the time variation of **Q** elements with data length of the adaptive **EKF** after **NIS** cost convergence. For a given manoeuvre in space, the choice of the coordinate system and hence the components along different axes could vary. Very rapid dynamics demand higher **Q** to track and slower dynamics demand lower **Q**. This leads to different overall constant **Q**s being injected in different state variables and thus the Kalman gains. In the same frame, if the origin is changed, trajectory can be hard or soft. For example, if initially the manoeuvre is very rapid in azimuth and elevation channels (with injected constant **Q**), the filter cannot track the **BR** closely, thus giving rise to oscillatory tracking error. Other axes systems and sensitivity studies for filter statistics are available in Sarkar [30].

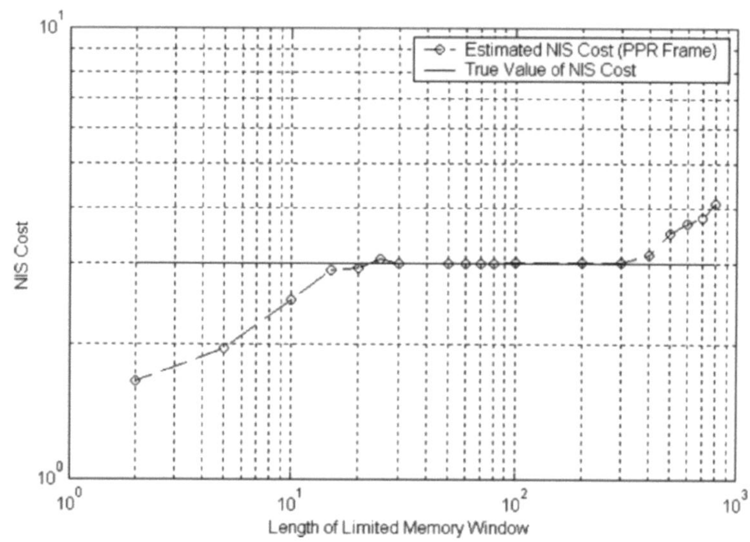

Figure 1.
Variation of the NIS cost with length of limited memory window.

4.4 Real-time tracking using CGKF

The small differences in the gains from **AEKF** and **CGKF** are due to the duration of the transient and the steady state. At first, a set of **R**, **A** and **E** measurements are generated for one launch angle of the **BR** (45°). This data set is processed using **AEKF** to estimate **P0**, **Q** and **R** adaptively by equating the **NIS** cost function to 3, the number of measurement channels. After some initial transients, the **Q** and **K** elements become constant as can be seen in **Figures 2** and **3**, respectively. The

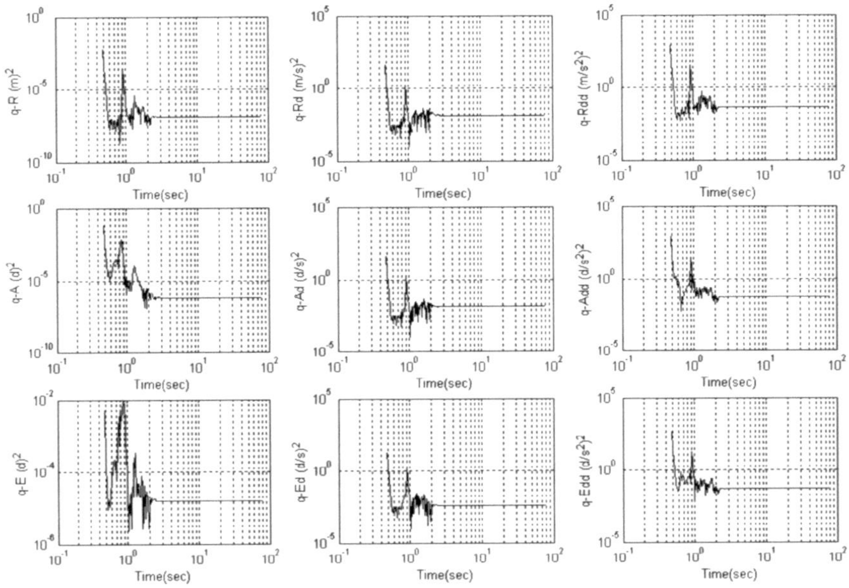

Figure 2.
Time variation of **Q** *elements with data length of the adaptive* **EKF** *after* **NIS** *cost convergence.*

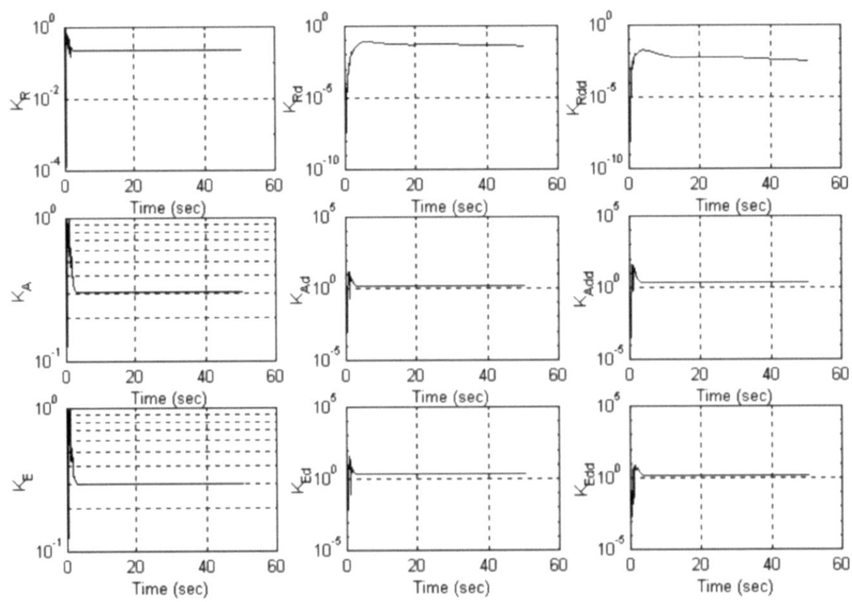

Figure 3.
Time variation of **K** *elements with data length of the adaptive* **EKF** *after* **NIS** *cost convergence.*

steady state gains from the **AEKF** for 45° are used for processing the real data for a different launch angle of 75° of the same **BR** and the filter performs well. This is because the **Q** values from **AEKF** for 45 and 70°, being only slightly different, do not affect the gains in **AEKF,** so also in **CGKF** and thereby the filter performance. The **NIS** cost function for **AEKF** based on **L** = 5 is 3.05. For αβγ filter, the combination of λ equal to (0.002, 0.001, 0.001); (0.02, 0.01, 0.01); (0.05, 0.02, 0.02); (0.07, 0.05, 0.05) and (0.1, 0.1, 0.1) gave costs of 56.0, 17.0, 5.71, 3.03 and 2.85, respectively. These indicate the αβγ filter and the constant gain **AEKF** performance are close when λ = (0.07, 0.05, 0.05). Thus, the choice of gain elements from **AEKF** and **CGKF** is better than in the αβγ filter and the latter is simpler to implement.

5. Space debris re-entry

An accurate prediction of re-entry time of large orbital space debris is useful to plan hazard assessment and mitigation strategies. The database for such an analysis of large objects is the set of two line elements (**TLEs**) provided by agencies like **USSPACECOM**. The **TLE** sets [49] provide information regarding orbital parameters together with rate of mean motion decay and a reference parameter $\mathbf{B}^*$ related to the ballistic coefficient **B** as

$$\mathbf{B}^* = (\boldsymbol{\rho}_o/2)\,\mathbf{B} = (\boldsymbol{\rho}_o/2)\,(\mathbf{C_D}\ \mathbf{A_{eff}}/\mathbf{m}) \tag{35}$$

B represents the sensitivity of an object to air drag and $\mathbf{B}^*$ is an adjusted value of **B** using the reference value of atmospheric density $\boldsymbol{\rho}_o$ at a reference altitude 120 km above earth. $\mathbf{C_D}$ is the non dimensional drag coefficient, **m** is the mass and $\mathbf{A_{eff}}$ is the effective area of cross-section of the object. Larger **B** means its orbit decays faster.

5.1 Re-entry case study of US Sat. No. 25947, Soyuz

The Satellite No. 25947 is a rocket body that has been the test case for the third **IADC** Re-entry campaign. The sets of 72 orbital elements were made available for re-entry prediction during February 2, 2000, to March 3, 2000.

5.2 Filter-world scenario: state equations

The measurements are available in terms of the orbital parameters the semimajor axis ‘a’ and the eccentricity ‘e’ in both the simulated cases and the tracked **TLE** elements. The state equations governing the state variables (a, e, **B**) are [29]

$$a_k = a_{k-1} + \Delta\, a_{k-1} + w_1 = a_{k-1} + \phi 1\,(a_{k-1}, e_{k-1})\,\mathbf{B}_{k-1} + w_1 \tag{36}$$

$$e_k = e_{k-1} + \Delta\, e_{k-1} + w_2 = e_{k-1} + \phi 2\,(a_{k-1}, e_{k-1})\,\mathbf{B}_{k-1} + w_2 \tag{37}$$

$$\mathbf{B}_{k-1} = \mathbf{B}_{k-1} + w_3 \tag{38}$$

where ϕ1 and ϕ2 are the functional forms of King-Hele [50] which depend on ballistic coefficient **B**, ‘a’ and ‘e’, and w_1, w_2 and w_3 are, respectively, the process noises. The subscript argument inside the brackets (•) denotes the time instant.

5.3 Filter-world scenario: measurement equations

But, in the filter implementation process, the transformed variables, namely the predicted apogee and perigee heights, are

$$(ha^-)_k = a_k\,(1 + e_k)\ and\ (hp^-)_k = a_k\,(1 - e_k) \tag{39}$$

The measurements at time t(k) are of the form

$$(ha^-)_k = (ha^-)_k + \mathrm{v}_1 \text{ and } (hp^-)_k = (hp^-)_k + \mathrm{v}_2 \tag{40}$$

where v_1 and v_2 are the measurement noises assumed to be white Gaussian with zero mean and covariance **R** assumed as constant. The predicted values of these heights in the state equations are updated by utilising the measured values *ha* and *hp*, respectively, the apogee height and the perigee height.

$$\begin{bmatrix} ha^+ \\ hp^+ \\ B^+ \end{bmatrix}_k = \begin{bmatrix} ha^- \\ hp^- \\ B^- \end{bmatrix}_k + \begin{bmatrix} k11 & k12 \\ k21 & k22 \\ k31 & k32 \end{bmatrix} \bullet \begin{bmatrix} ha - ha^- \\ hp - hp^- \end{bmatrix}_k \tag{41}$$

The superscripts (+) and (−) correspond to the predicted and updated values, and suffix k denotes the time instant. Further details are available in Anilkumar [26] and Anilkumar et al. [29].

5.4 Uncertainties in the state and measurement equations requiring Q and R

In general, the physical parameters like mass, shape and dimensions of the re-entry objects that vary are not available accurately. Also, the atmosphere varies randomly. Further, the tumbling effect of the body and the molecule gas surface interaction leads to uncertain and varying aerodynamic drag coefficient, which makes the prediction of re-entry time a difficult problem. The re-entry objects are mainly affected by the atmospheric drag, earth's oblateness, solar activity index $F_{10.7}$ and magnetic index Ap. However, the orbital propagator utilised in this study is a very simple model of King-Hele [50] which accounts for only the atmospheric drag effect. The present propagator assumes a mean atmospheric condition as provided by the US Standard Atmosphere [51]. This model estimates only the semimajor axis and eccentricity decay with respect to one revolution, assuming a constant scale height during one revolution. This model is sufficient for the re-entry prediction as the decay of the object is mainly governed by the air drag only. The effects of other orbital perturbations and variations in the atmospheric density are accountable through the process noise and the Kalman filter is thus able to handle it through the proper gains as will be demonstrated subsequently. In all the prediction exercises, when the semimajor axis of the object reaches a height of 120 km above the earth, it is considered to have re-entered the atmosphere. This assumption is appropriate as a reference condition since there are significant variations in the atmospheric properties above 120 km with solar, magnetic activity and local time than below this height. Also, effectively, a diffusive equilibrium predominates beyond 120 km as given in Whitten et al. [52].

5.5 Adaptive filtering approach for re-entry prediction

It was found to be adequate to obtain **P0** based on the difference between the assumed initial conditions of the states (a, e) with those from the first **TLE** set. For state **B**, the deviation of initially assumed **B0** with that of the derived value of **B** from **B*** is used. For **Q** and **R**, the heuristic estimators of Myers and Tapley [15] have been used. A careful study of data of varying length based on adaptive filtering (both by simulation and actual data) helped to assess how the estimated

B, **Q** and **R** vary with data length. Recently, the **RRR** [6–9] has found a near optimal solution for tuning the filter statistics and thus an improvement over earlier adaptive procedures.

5.6 The CGKF approach for re-entry prediction

The present study utilised the genetic algorithm (**GA**) in the **CGKF** to minimise the cost function **J**. The fundamentals of **GA**, its features and other implementation aspects can be found in [39, 40]. The values of the parameters arrived at after some trials for the present **GA** re-entry problem are: population size = 100; bit length = 20; probability of cross over = 0.90; probability of mutation = 0.05; number of generations for convergence = 50 and tolerance for convergence: change in cost function **J** between generations = 0.0001.

Starting from the 22nd **TLE** set, the present constant gain Kalman filter algorithm utilises a total of six gains corresponding to the three states, namely, apogee and perigee heights and the ballistic coefficient and two apogee and perigee height measurements. An important parameter in this implementation is the initial assumed value of ballistic coefficient **B0.** This is to be expected as the body may be tumbling, with irregular shape and with varying gas molecule and surface interaction reflected in the predicted ballistic coefficient. Further, for the drag, a very simple mean atmospheric condition is used. **Figure 4** shows that as time passes, with more and more **TLE** data sets being available, for various initial **B0** values, the predicted re-entry date comes closer. But the point is what is the best choice for the initial **B0** that provides minimum variation in the predicted re-entry time right from the beginning up to the actual re-entry? This turns out to be **B0** = 0.40 as shown in **Figure 5**. The overall problem is to find out the best possible **B0** and the constant Kalman gain that predicts the re-entry time with least variation from the beginning to the end.

A combination of adaptive filtering and the constant gain approaches provided a set of constant gains as [0.6, 0.2, 0.2, 0.6, 0.00014 and 0.0001], as nearly optimal [26, 29]. One curious fact that may be noticed is the choice of the optimum Kalman gains. The optimal gain values for the states are larger and for **B** it is very small, the reason being the noise-to-signal ratio is very small for the states. Hence, the filter

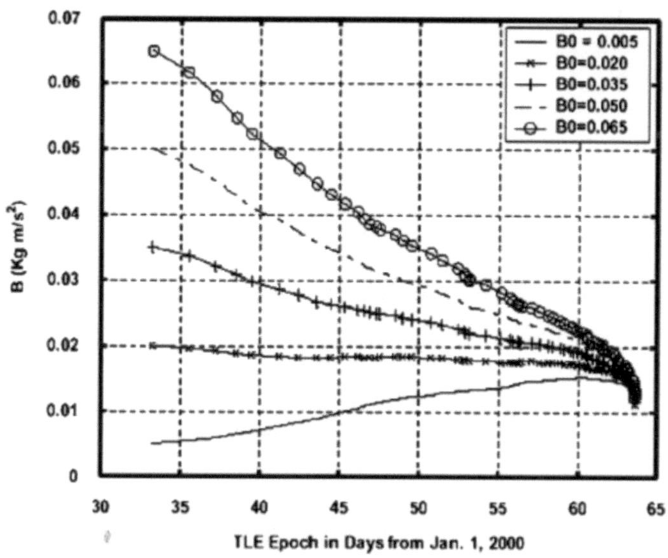

Figure 4.
*Variation of **B** with time during re-entry.*

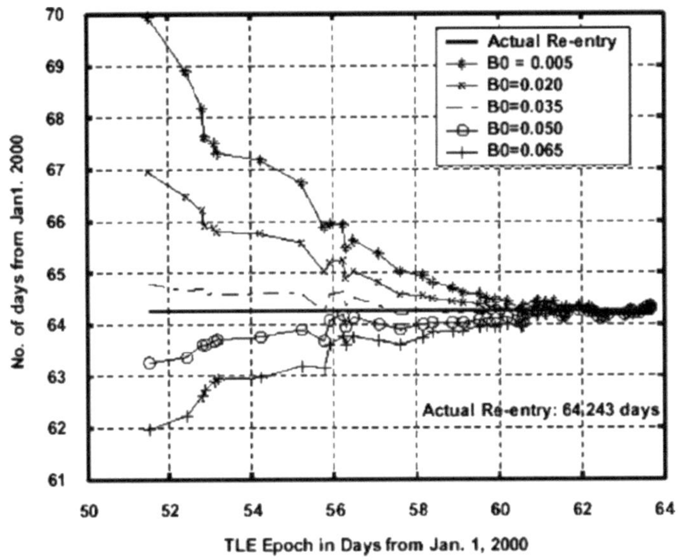

Figure 5.
Variation of re-entry time with **Bo**.

can track the state with a large gain value close to unity or even a small non-zero value (but not zero!). However, for the ballistic coefficient **B**, the gains have to be smaller in order to slowly learn from the measurements; and if these gains are larger, then the estimated **B** will show lot of fluctuations. The actual re-entry occurred on March 4, 2000, at 5 h 50 min. The **CGKF** formalism based on a mean atmosphere and approximate drag effects predicted the re-entry on March 4, 2000, at 5 h 35 min. Even the MSIS-86 model [53] could have been used. This shows once again the robustness of the constant gains has the ability to handle the inaccuracies in modelling **B**, as well as both the unmodelled and unmodellable state and measurement noise characteristics.

6. Evolution and expansion of the space debris scenario

6.1 Introduction

The evolution of the space debris scenario consisting of characterising each and every fragment can be very unwieldy. The purpose of the present study is to demonstrate that it is not necessary to follow each and every fragment in a complex environment, which demands enormous amount of computing time. It suffices to group the fragments called equivalent fragments (**EQF**) in the 'a', 'e' coarse bins and propagate these with time. However, the orbital and ballistic coefficients of the **EQF**s need to be redefined for the above purpose of time propagation in terms of the individual fragment characteristics constituting it. After time propagation, the number of fragments and their ballistic coefficient constituting the **EQF**s are updated based on just the measured number of individual fragments as will be explained later. This process is continued with subsequent measurements.

For studying the long-term evolution of the space debris, an initial model like in Johnson and McKnight [54], **ASSEMBLE** model of Anilkumar et al. [27], and Rossi et al. [55] can be assumed. At large times, the prediction could depart greatly from the real scenario due to the sensitivity of the evolution to the inaccuracies in the model parameters and the environment. There are large differences in the estimated characteristics among many debris models [26, 54]. The only way the prediction can be made to follow more closely the real situation is to update the characteristics by assimilating properly the subsequent measurements of the number density in (a, e) bins repeatedly for further evolution in time. The present procedure in addition also expands the scenario for the distribution of the ballistic coefficient of the debris as well(!) which is not generally available or measurable.

6.2 The present approach and the stochastic analog tool of Rossi et al.

The stochastic analog tool (**STAT**) of Rossi et al. [55] simulates the time evolution of the debris by a threefold subdivision of namely: (i) the semimajor axis 'a' from 6378 to 46,378 km, (ii) the eccentricity 'e' from 0 to 1 and (iii) the mass 'm' from 1 mg to 10,000 kg. The present approach considers a, log(e) and log(B) as against a, e and m of **STAT**. The third parameter **B** has been presently used because the orbital parameters are sensitive to the air drag and thus change with time. There are errors due to discretisation and approximation in specifying the arithmetic mean values for 'a' and geometric values 'e' of the **EQF** in the various bins. Further, there are unaccounted or even unmodellable forces during propagation. However, all such errors can be accounted for by process noise in the state equations describing the propagation of the **EQF**. Since the individual representative objects of each bin are propagated, the computing time is almost independent of the debris population size in both the present and **STAT** approaches. It is the second step that is fundamentally new and different in the present approach namely at an update apart from assimilating the measurement information it also expands the scenario to update the equivalent ballistic coefficient (**EQB**) for the **EQF**s in various bins with time.

6.2.1 Characteristics of the equivalent fragment (EQF) in terms of the fragments in a bin

Presently, with 10 divisions for each of the parameters a, e and **B**, a total of 1000 bins are formed. Instead of handling each and every fragment, the fragments in every bin are handled as a fewer number of **EQFs**. Next, to follow the dynamics of these **EQFs**, it is necessary to assign suitable orbital and ballistic coefficient values for these **EQFs** in terms of the individual fragment properties. Presently, these are set as the arithmetic mean for 'a', geometric mean for 'e' and the geometric mean also for '**B**' of the number of fragments in each bin. As the **EQFs** meander across the various '**B'** bins, their ballistic coefficients are updated. This is somewhat similar to a debris with a certain value of **B** moving in the atmosphere though it could change its value. A priori, how well a mean defined as above can follow the dynamics and subsequently get updated in the filter is not conceptually clear. Its adequacy can only be demonstrated from subsequent results.

6.2.2 Evolution of individual fragments as well as EQF in the bins

Initially, about 10,000 simulated debris fragments due to an explosion are considered and the later fragments due to further breakups are accounted for as source terms. The state propagation equations for both the fragments and the **EQF** are identical to the earlier Eqs. (38), (39) and (40). The **EQF** propagated based on its assigned value of suitable 'a' and 'e' and could in general end up in just within another bin. In order to redistribute the fraction of the **EQFs** among the bins, a heuristic rule is used as in Rossi et al. [55] that takes the ratio between the area covered by the propagated rectangle and the area of the initial rectangle as shown in **Figure 6**.

Subsequently, by using the measurements of the number of debris in the bins at various times, the **EQB** of each **EQF** is updated based on the weighted average of

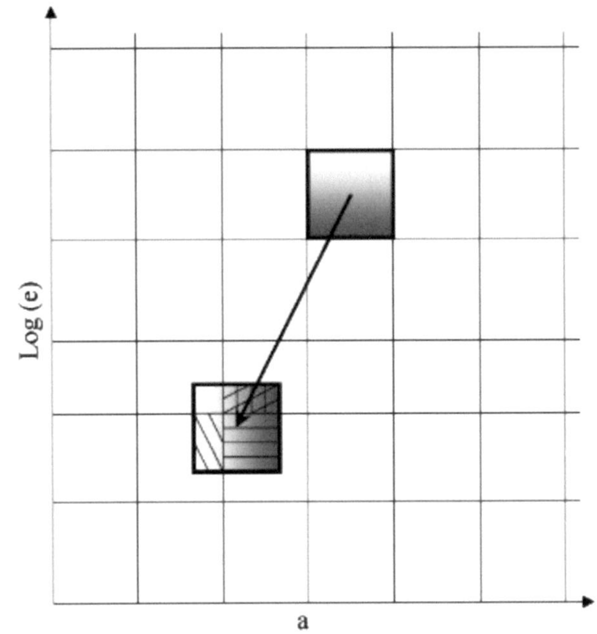

Figure 6.
Representation of the orbital propagation and redistribution in the eccentricity 'e' versus semimajor axis 'a' space.

the predicted and measured number density of the fragments in the bins. This weightage is the Kalman gain as we will see later on. Without the update of the **EQB** of these **EQF**, the filter is unable to follow the true time variation of the number density of the debris fragments in the bins. Hence, the ballistic coefficient of the **EQF** is aptly called as the **EQB**.

6.2.3 Update of the EQF characteristics

The evolution of the **EQF** takes place in two steps, namely: (i) the propagation of the **EQF**s representing all the fragments in the various bins, then, redistribution of the fragments around the adjacent bins as mentioned earlier; further breakups are also accounted for by the changed number density in the various bins, and (ii) using appropriate constant Kalman gains for obtaining an updated estimate of the number density of the fragments in the various bins and the **EQB** of the **EQF**s.

There is one subtle point in the estimation of the **EQB** of the **EQF** corresponding to various (a, e) bins. After update, the value of **B** for the **EQB** of **EQF** at times can fall outside the fixed bin interval. Presently, we have taken the propagation of the **EQF** always from the initial (a, e) condition based on the arithmetic and geometric mean, respectively. But, for a group of fragments, the above initial condition may not be the most appropriate. The **EQF** could have started its trajectory from anywhere inside or on the boundary of (a, e) bin whence the redistribution could have been different and thus the updated ballistic coefficient **B** as well. Such features arise due to the definition of the **EQF** characteristics and the coarseness of the bins, but one has to see if the final results are meaningful and acceptable.

6.2.4 Real-world (individual fragments) and filter-world (EQF) scenarios

The state and measurement equations in the real-world and filter-world scenarios are given in **Table 3**. In the filter state equations, the binning, formation

Quantity	Real World Scenario for each fragment	Filter World Scenario for each EQF
The state variables	The (a, e, **B**) of each fragment.	The (a, e, **B**) of each **EQF**.
The initial conditions	The initial (a, e) of each fragment.	For the **EQF** from anywhere in the (a, e) bin.
The state input	Complex environment.	Only the air drag effect is considered.
The state process	Random variations in the real environment.	The inaccuracies in assigning (a, e, **B**), binning, its propagation, redistribution and the environment.
The measured variables	The number of individual fragments in the various bins.	The **EQFs** are propagated with only air drag and later converted to the number of objects in each of the bins.
The measurement noise	Measurement errors due to tracking and data processing.	No measurement noise as the **EQFs** are propagated and using the changed values of (a, e) are assigned to appropriate bins.

Table 3.
Real world without binning and filter world with binning (for simulation studies).

of **EQF**, propagation and redistribution all lead to modelling error and need process noise to handle the situation. In a real-world scenario, there would be measurement noise due to inaccuracies in the assigned orbital characteristics of the individual fragments. In simulation studies, the propagation of each and every one of the individual debris fragments and counting their number in the various bins lead to no measurement noise.

The uncertainties in the initial **EQB** values of the **EQF** in the state equations (shown in **Table 3**) are improved by the filter by using a certain length of data. In the present study, the constant Kalman gains have been derived as explained later.

6.3 The present constant gain Kalman filter approach

From simulated studies, the number of debris fragments in each three-dimensional (a, e, **B**) bin is known exactly. The Kalman filter by using the constant gains and the updated number of objects at various times is able to track closely the true number of fragments. Similarly, the measurements can be assimilated and the scenario expanded to get the **EQB**.

6.3.1 Filter-world state equations

Thus, the states presently considered in every one of the (a, e) bins are the number of objects **N** and their **EQB**. The (a, e) bins are not changing and the **EQF** moves in the (a, e) plane like any other single fragment and later gets redistributed based on a certain rule. The various **EQFs** are specified by: (i) their number in each (a, e) bin; (ii) the equivalent semimajor axis, (iii) the equivalent eccentricity and (iv) the **EQB**.

The state equations for the **EQF** in the various bins between measurements are

$$\begin{aligned} d\mathbf{N}/dt = {} & \Sigma[\text{propagation across the } (a, e) \text{ bins and redistribution} + \text{source terms}] \\ & + \text{state noise} \end{aligned} \tag{42}$$

$$d\mathbf{B}/dt = 0 + \text{state noise } (= 0) \tag{43}$$

6.3.2 Filter-world measurement update equations

The true number density $\mathbf{N_M}$ in the various bins is obtained in simulation by propagating each and every individual debris fragment. This is used to update the predicted number density based on propagated and redistributed **EQF** as well as update the ballistic coefficient of the **EQF** in the various bins as given by

$$\mathbf{N}^{+} = \mathbf{N}^{-} + \mathbf{K_N}.\,(\mathbf{N_M} - \mathbf{N}^{-}); \tag{44}$$

$$\mathbf{B}^{+} = \mathbf{B}^{-} + \mathbf{K_B}.(\mathbf{N_M} - \mathbf{N}^{-}) \tag{45}$$

with the pre- and post-updated values denoted, respectively, by the superscripts (−) and (+). The gains $\mathbf{K_N}$ and $\mathbf{K_B}$, respectively, correspond to the number density and the equivalent ballistic coefficient.

Presently, the number of constant gains $\mathbf{K_N}$ and $\mathbf{K_B}$ to be estimated is 200 with two for each of the 100 (a, e) bins. These are obtained based on minimising the cost function.

$$\mathbf{J} = (\mathbf{1/N})\boldsymbol{\Sigma}\boldsymbol{\nu}_\mathbf{k}\,[\mathcal{R}]^{-\mathbf{1}}\boldsymbol{\nu}_\mathbf{k}^{\mathrm{T}} \tag{46}$$

$\boldsymbol{\Sigma}$ denotes the summation over all bins and times. The constant Kalman gains were obtained by using the genetic algorithm [39, 40]. The different parameters used in **GA** implementation are as follows: population size = 200; bit length = 20; probability of cross over = 0.90; probability of mutation = 0.05; Convergence: number of generations 50 or alternately change in **J** between generations 0.0001.

The whole of Kalman filter process can be summed up in a simple way. One can have the evolution of the state (without knowing how) generated by any random process. The time variation of the state can even be assumed to be given. The measurements could be noisy or even exact. In order to track the state and also follow it smoothly by reducing the fluctuations, a simple filter can be designed with the states remaining constant between measurements. For zero Kalman gain, the filter will learn nothing from the measurements and the state will remain at the initial values. For unity Kalman gain, the state will follow the measurements. In between, there is a range of gain for which the difference between the predicted state and the measurement is minimised in a suitable sense over the range of data. For slow and fast state dynamics, gains near zero and unity, respectively, would be appropriate. Further, if the random process is known to have an inaccurate or unknown parameter, they can also be handled by additional constant gains.

6.3.3 Evolution of debris objects generated due to explosions

A single explosion at a typical altitude of 800 km and eccentricity 0.00045 resulting in about 10,000 debris of varying ballistic coefficients is simulated using the **ASSEMBLE** model [26, 27]. These objects were propagated accounting for only the atmospheric drag effect for a period of 600 days and thus generate the (a, e, **B**) data of the objects. Among many studies, updating both the number of objects and the **EQB** gave the best results and is described here for brevity. Further experiments like initial explosion followed by one breakup, two break ups and some launch activities were carried out. The filtering process reduces the errors in the estimates, but not below a certain value due to continuous occurrence of error due to binning, propagation and redistribution leading to a non-zero **K**. In all the subsequent figures, the symbol (o) denotes the true, (solid line) filter and (dashed line) with no update using **K** = 0.

6.3.4 Evolution of a single breakup and additional debris

Figure 7 provides the results by updating both the number density and the **EQB** for the typical B bin (0.6056, 1.6476). **Figure 8** shows the variation of the constant Kalman gain $\mathbf{K_N}$ across the semimajor axes bins for four ballistic bins are always between zero and unity since the state, namely the number density, is measured.

Figure 9 shows the $\mathbf{K_B}$ for various values of the semimajor axes bins. However, this takes positive and negative values. Such a thing can happen since the ballistic coefficient though a state has not been measured. Further, in other experiments that were performed, it was noted that the estimated ballistic coefficient with time in typical bins is generally within the limits of the ballistic coefficient bin values. However, at times, they move somewhat outside the limits of the bin values. The initial condition for **EQF** propagation from the mean values of the bins, though it could have started from anywhere inside the bins, the subsequent propagation and redistribution error could be responsible for such a behaviour. It is best to accept the approach here as the ability to mimic the dynamical behaviour.

At the beginning 10,000 fragments were introduced and subsequently an additional 300 fragments were introduced after 120 days very much like the real-world scenario where the debris are growing but not too rapidly. Even after adding the new source terms, the constant Kalman gains obtained based on the initial cloud evolution have been used for further evolution. In general, the constant gains are robust around a range of the estimated values. Hence, even if the subsequent results are non-optimal, they are adequate to obtain acceptable estimates.

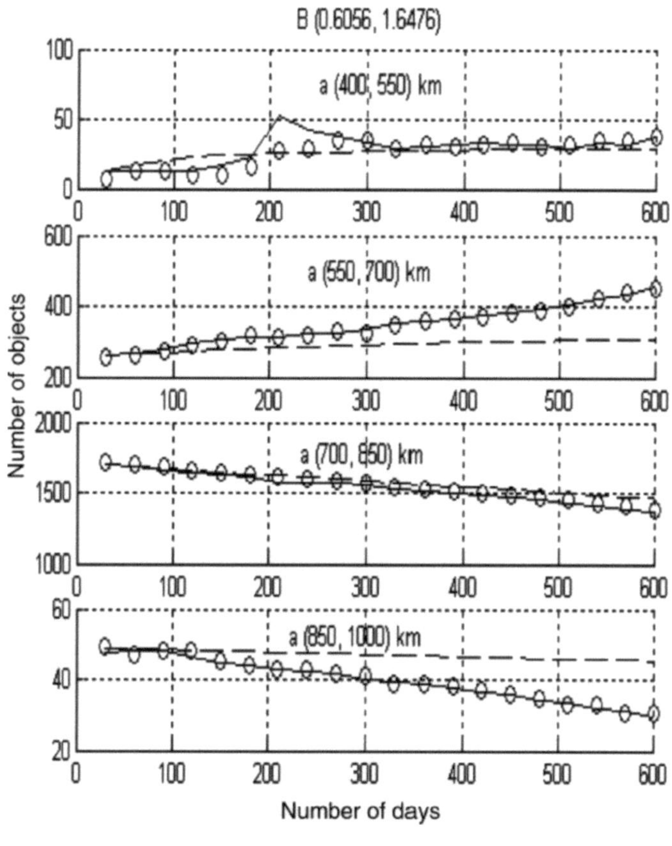

Figure 7.
Breakup evolution in B bin (0.6056, 1.6476).

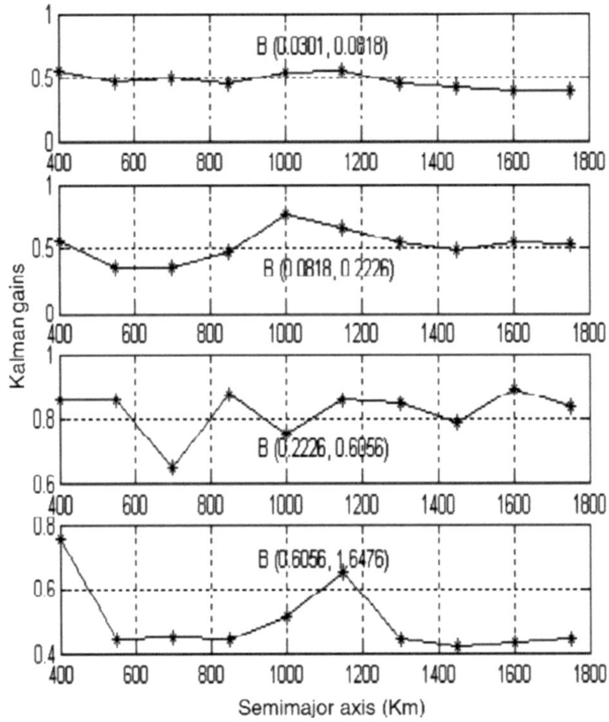

Figure 8.
Kalman gains for number of objects (K_N).

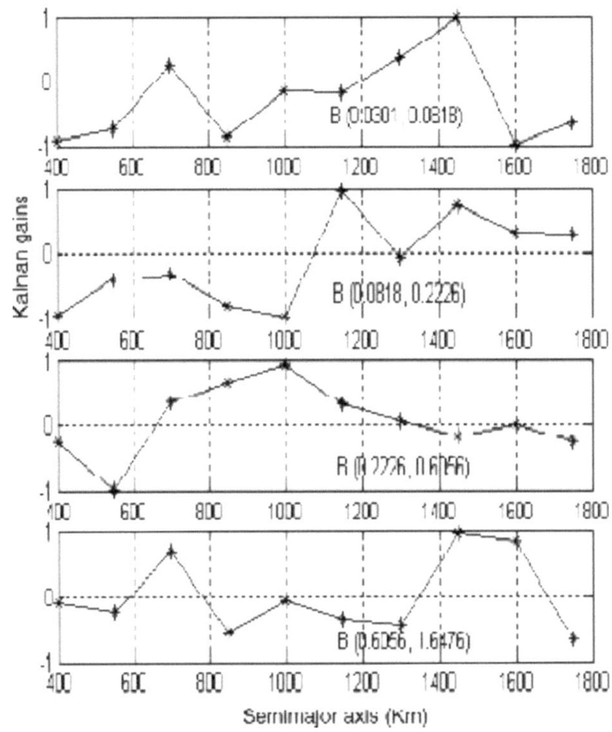

Figure 9.
Kalman gains for ballistic coefficients (K_B).

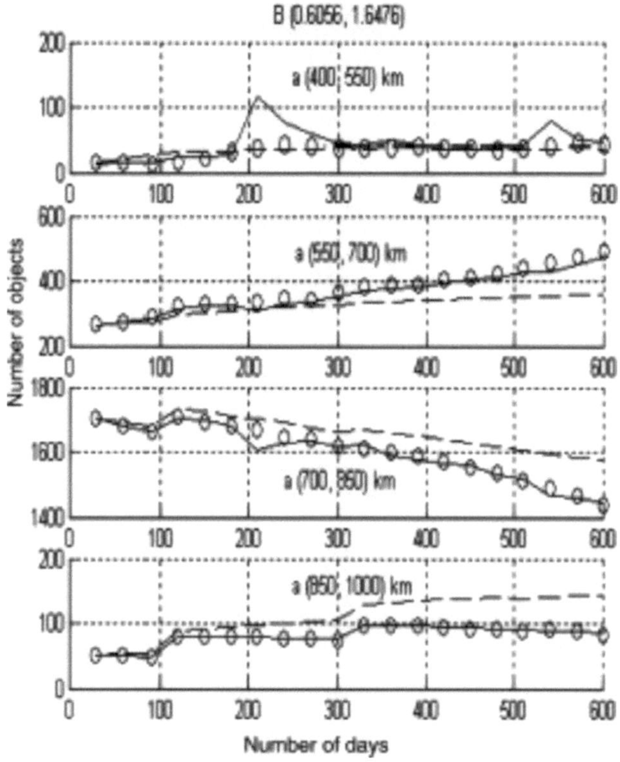

Figure 10.
Estimated and observed number of objects. (Two explosions and some new launches).

6.3.5 Evolution of a single breakup followed by more than one breakup and some launch activities

To simulate the real-world scenario, two explosions and some launches are introduced during the evolution. Once again, the constant gains obtained using the primary debris clouds suffice for all later cases as well! The results provided in **Figure 10** show that the present model is able to track the number of objects even in such evolution process.

6.3.6 Application to a typical real-world scenario

The catalogued **TLE** data of 335 debris objects in near circular orbits in the perigee and apogee bin of 700–800 km from October 1998 to September 1999 were chosen, assuming an initial ballistic coefficient for the **EQF**s is propagated and updated using first eight observations. A constant eccentricity for all the EQFs in all the bins is assumed since the bin size is just 10 km (unlike in the simulated scenario where it was 150) km but their semimajor axis corresponds to the mid-value of the bin. The Kalman gains from simulation studies were once again used to analyse the real-world data(!), thus demonstrating the robustness of the constant Kalman gains. The innovation here is given by the difference between the **TLE** data and the predicted number density. The 335 objects observed in the apogee/perigee bin from October 1998 were tracked for the next 12 months to obtain the number of objects in the semimajor axis bins. By tracking the same objects, **Figure 11** provides their number for the 12 months in the 10 different semimajor axis bins.

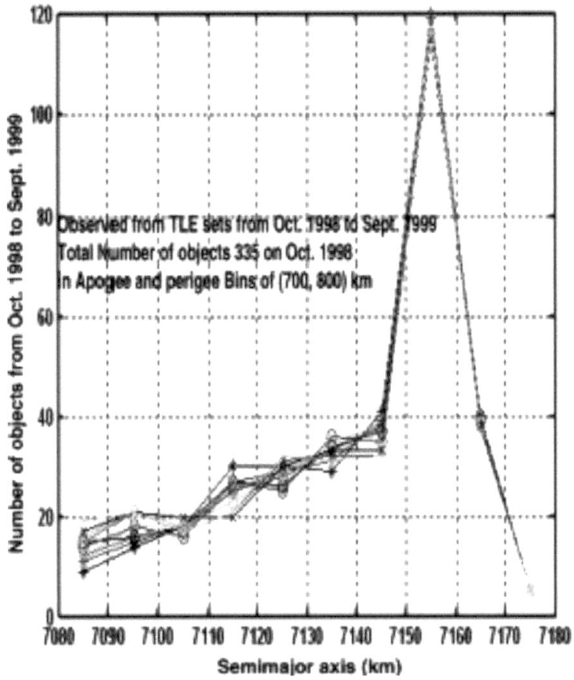

Figure 11.
Variation of the number density of the debris in the bins with time.

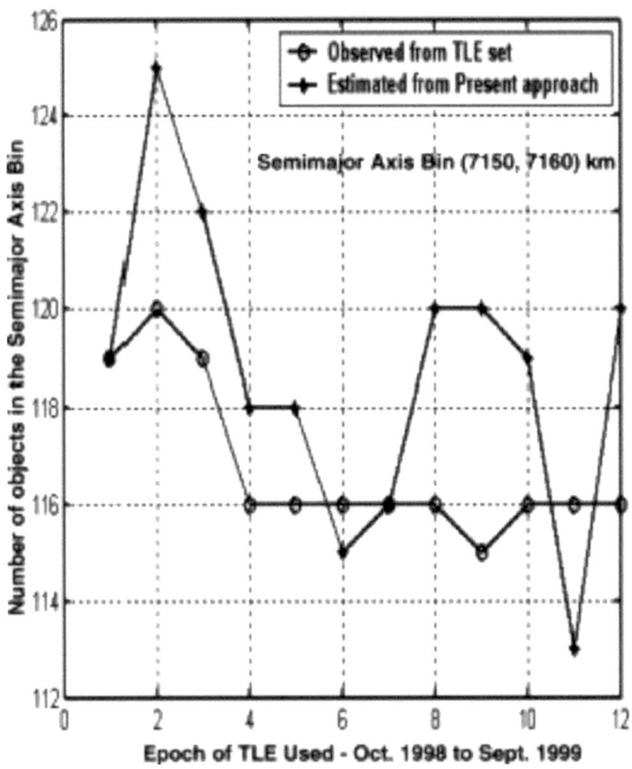

Figure 12.
Comparison of the estimated time-varying debris number density with TLE values.

Figure 12 shows a comparison of the number of objects from the present approach with that observed for the semimajor axis bin of (7150, 7160) km. Considering 10 equivalent objects rather than propagating and monitoring all of the 335 objects, the match is quite good.

7. Conclusions

The present **CGKF** approach has been demonstrated with many examples and in particular the evolution of thousands of space debris fragments. This formalism can be used even in massive atmospheric data assimilation and weather prediction problems that have tens of thousands of states and measurements.

Acknowledgements

The author sincerely thanks all collaborators referred to in this chapter. It has been very kind of Prof. Felix Govaers to have invited me to contribute a chapter in this book and also to INTECHOPEN for publishing it.

Author details

Mudambi R. Ananthasayanam
Department of Aerospace Engineering, Indian Institute of Science, Bangalore, India

*Address all correspondence to: sayanam2005@yahoo.co.in

References

[1] Kalman RE. A new approach to linear filtering and prediction problems. Transactions of the ASME - Journal of Basic Engineering. 1960;**82**(Series D): 35-45

[2] Brown R, Hwang P. Introduction to Random Signals and Applied Kalman Filtering, with MATLAB Exercises. 4th ed. John Wiley and Sons; 2012

[3] Kailath T. An innovations approach to least-squares estimation part I: Linear filtering in additive white noise. IEEE Transactions on Automatic Control. 2016;**13**(6):646-655

[4] Klein V, Morelli EA. Aircraft System Identification: Theory and Practice. AIAA Edn. Series; 2006

[5] Jategaonkar RV. Flight Vehicle System Identification: A Time Domain Methodology. Vol. 216. AIAA; 2006

[6] Shyam MM, Naik N, Gemson RMO, Ananthasayanam MR. Introduction to the Kalman filter and tuning its statistics for near optimal estimates and Cramer Rao bound, TR/EE2015/401; IIT Kanpur; 2015. Available from: http://arxiv.org/abs/1503.04313

[7] Ananthasayanam MR, Shyam Mohan M, Naik N, Gemson RMO. A heuristic reference recursive recipe for adaptively tuning the Kalman filter statistics part-1: Formulation and simulation studies. Sadhana. 2016;**41**(12):1473-1490

[8] Shyam Mohan M, Naik N, Gemson RMO, Ananthasayanam MR. A heuristic reference recursive recipe for adaptively tuning the Kalman filter statistics part-2: Real data studies. Sadhana. 2016;**41**(12): 1491-1507

[9] Ananthasayanam MR. A reference recursive recipe for tuning the statistics of the Kalman filter. In: de Oliveira Serra GL, editor. Kalman Filters-Theory for Advanced Applications, INTECHOPEN. DOI: 10.5772/intechopen.71961

[10] Narasimha R. Performance reliability of high maintenance systems. Journal of the Franklin Institute. 1975; **303**:15-29

[11] Ananthasayanam MR. A relook at the concepts and competence of the Kalman filter. In: Proceedings of the 42nd AIAA Aerospace Sciences Meeting and Exhibit; 5-8 January 2004; Reno, Nevada. AIAA-2004-571

[12] Ananthasayanam MR. Fascinating perspectives of state and parameter estimation techniques, AIAA-2000-4319

[13] Sorenson HW. Least squares estimation from Gauss to Kalman. IEEE Spectrum. 1970;7:63-68

[14] Mehra R. Approaches to adaptive filtering. IEEE Transactions on Automatic Control. 1972;**17**:903-908

[15] Myers KA, Tapley BD. Adaptive sequential estimation with unknown noise statistics. IEEE Transactions on Automatic Control. 1976;**21**:520-525

[16] Gemson RMO. Estimation of aircraft aerodynamic derivatives accounting for measurement and process noise by EKF through adaptive filter tuning [PhD thesis]. Bangalore, India: Department of Aerospace Engineering, Indian Institute of Science; 1991

[17] Gemson RMO, Ananthasayanam MR. Importance of initial state covariance matrix for the parameter estimation using adaptive extended Kalman filter. In: Proceedings of AIAA Atmospheric Flight Mechanics, AIAA-98-4153. 1998. pp. 94-104

[18] Wilson KC. An optimal control approach to designing constant gain filters. IEEE Transactions on Aerospace and Electronic Systems. 1972;**8**(6): 836-842

[19] Cook G, Dawson DE. Optimum constant-gain filters. IEEE Transactions on Industrial Electronics and Control Instrumentation, IEEE. 1974

[20] Grimble MJ, Jukes KA, Goodall DP. Nonlinear filters and operators and the constant-gain extended Kalman filter. IMA Journal of Mathematical Control and Information. 1984;**1**:359-386

[21] Kobayashi T. Application of a constant gain extended Kalman filter for in-flight estimation of aircraft engine performance parameters, NASA/TM—2005-213865. 2005

[22] Liu X, Yu Y, Li Z, Iu HHC, Fernando T. A novel constant gain Kalman filter design for nonlinear systems. Signal Processing. DOI: 10.1016/j.sigpro.2017.01.002

[23] Song TL, Speyer JL. A stochastic analysis of a modified gain extended Kalman filter with applications to estimation with bearing only measurements. IEEE Transactions on Automatic Control. 1985;(10):940-949

[24] Gelb A. Applied Optimal Estimation. Cambridge, Massachusetts, MIT Press; 1974

[25] Sugiyama N. System identification of jet engines. Journal of Engineering for Gas Turbines and Power. 2000;**122**: 19-26

[26] Anilkumar AK. New perspectives for analyzing the breakup, environment, evolution, collision risk and reentry of space debris objects [PhD thesis]. India: Department of Aerospace Engineering, Indian Institute of Science; 2004

[27] Anilkumar AK, Ananthasayanam MR, Subba Rao PV. A posterior semi-stochastic low earth debris on-orbit breakup simulation model. Acta Astronautica. 2005;**57**:733-746

[28] Ananthasayanam MR, Anilkumar AK, Subba Rao PV. New approach for the evolution and expansion of space debris scenario. Journal of Spacecraft and Rockets. 2006;**43**(6):1271-1282

[29] Anilkumar AK, Ananthasayanam MR, Subba Rao PV. A constant gain Kalman filter approach for the prediction of re-entry of risk objects. Acta Astronautica. 2007;**61**:831-839

[30] Sarkar AK. New perspectives in state and parameter estimation of flight vehicles for off line and real time applications [PhD thesis]. Bangalore, India: Department of Aerospace Engineering, Indian Institute of Science; 2004

[31] Viswanath. Study of constant gain Kalman filter for basic systems with preliminary study of ISAR problem [MTech thesis]. India: IIT Kanpur; 2018

[32] Philip NK. A study of the estimation schemes with controller for the final phase of a rendezvous and docking mission of spacecraft [PhD thesis]. Bangalore, India: Department of Aerospace Engineering, Indian Institute of Science; 2001

[33] Philip NK, Ananthasayanam MR. Relative position and attitude estimation and control schemes for the final phase of an autonomous docking mission of spacecraft. Acta Astronautica. 2003;**52**: 511-522

[34] Anand Raj R. Kalman filter estimation of ionospheric tec and differential instrumental biases over low latitude using dual frequency GPS observations [MSc thesis]. Bangalore, India: Department of Aerospace

Engineering, Indian Institute of Science; 2006

[35] Anandraj R, Ananthasayanam MR, Mahapatra PR, Soma P. Estimation of Low Latitude Ionospheric TEC from Dual Frequency GPS Observations by Using Adaptive Kalman Filtering Technique. Chicago: International Union of Radio Science. Union Radio Scientifique Internationale. XXIX General Assembly; 2008

[36] Basil H. Studies on a low cost integrated navigation system using MEMS-INS and GPS with adaptive and constant gain Kalman filters [MSc thesis]. Bangalore, India: Department of Aerospace Engineering, Indian Institute of Science; 2005

[37] Basil H, Ananthasayanam MR, Puri SN. An application of constant Kalman gain approach for the problem of integrating the MEMS-INS and the GPS, JS-65. In: KSAS-JSASS Joint Symposium; Seoul, Korea; 2004

[38] Yadav A, Naik N, Ananthasayanam MR, Gaur A, Singh YN. A constant gain Kalman filter approach to target tracking in wireless sensor networks. In: Industrial and Information Systems (ICIIS), 2012 7th IEEE International Conference on. pp. 1-7

[39] Deb K. Optimization for Engineering Design: Algorithms and Examples. Prentice-Hall of India; 1995

[40] Goldberg DE. Genetic Algorithms in Search, Optimization & Machine Learning. Addison-Wesley; 2000

[41] Billard R. Aryabhata and Indian Astronomy. Indian Journal of History of Science. 1977;**12**(2):207-224

[42] Billard R. L'astronomie Indienne. Paris: Publications De Ecole Francaise D'Extreme-Orient; 1971

[43] Sarma KV. Tradition of Aryabhatiya in Kerala: Revision of planetary parameters. Indian Journal of History of Science. 1977;**12**(2):194-199

[44] Maine RE, Iliff KW. Programmer's manual for MMLE3, a general Fortran program for maximum likelihood parameter estimation, NASA TP-1690. 1981

[45] Blair WD. Fixed-gain, two-stage estimators for tracking maneuvering targets. Report No. NSWCDD/TR-92/297. 1992

[46] Bar-Shalom Y, Rong Li X, Kirubarajan T. Estimation with Applications to Tracking and Navigation, Theory, Algorithm and Software. John Wiley and Sons; 2000

[47] Mehrotra K, Mahapatra PR. A jerk model for tracking highly maneuvering targets. IEEE Transactions on Aerospace and Electronic Systems. 1997;**33**(4): 1094-1105

[48] Singer RA. Estimating optimal tracking filter performance for manned maneuvering targets. IEEE Transactions on Aerospace and Electronic Systems. 1970;**6**:473-483

[49] Web sites for two line element (TLE) sets. Available from: (http://www.geocities.com/iss25544/#TLEs) or (www.wingar.demon.co.uk) or (http://www.celestrak.com)

[50] King-Hele D. Satellite Orbits in an Atmosphere: Theory and Applications. London: Blackie; 1987

[51] NOAA, NASA and USAF, U.S. US Standard Atmosphere. Washington, DC: Government Printing Offices; 1976

[52] Whitten RC, Vaughan WW. Guide to Reference and Standard Atmosphere Models, AIAA-G-003-1988. 1990

[53] Hedin AE. MSIS-86 thermospheric model. Journal of Geophysical Research. 1987;**92**:4649-4662

[54] Johnson NL, McKnight DS. Artificial Space Debris. Orbit Book Company; 1987

[55] Rossi A, Cordelli A, Farinella P, Anselmo L. Collisional evolution of the earth's orbital debris cloud. Journal of Geophysical Research. 1994;**99**(E11): 23195-23210

Chapter 4

Statically Fused Converted Measurement Kalman Filters

Gongjian Zhou and Zhengkun Guo

Abstract

This chapter presents a state estimation method without using of nonlinear recursive filters when Doppler measurement is incorporated into the tracking system. The commonly used motions, such as the constant velocity (CV), constant acceleration (CA), and constant turn (CT), are represented in a pseudo-state space, defined from the product of target true range and range rate, by linear pseudo-state equations. Then the linear converted Doppler measurement Kalman filter (CDMKF) is presented to extract pseudo-state from the converted Doppler measurement, constructed by the product of the range and Doppler measurements. The output of the CDMKF is fused statically with that of the converted position measurement (range and one or two angles) Kalman filter (CPMKF) to produce target Cartesian state estimates. The accuracy and consistence of the estimator can be both guaranteed, since linear Kalman filters are both used to extract information from position and Doppler measurements.

Keywords: Kalman filter, measurement conversion, doppler, static fusion

1. Introduction

In real tracking applications, most sensors report target parameters in sensor (e.g., polar) coordinates, while target motion is usually modeled in Cartesian coordinates. In Doppler radars, the measurements consist of range, one or two angles, and range rate. Tracking in Cartesian coordinates using polar measurements is a nonlinear estimation problem. To handle the range and angle measurements, it is preferred to convert the measurements to a linear form in Cartesian coordinates to avoid nonlinear filtering. This results in the converted position measurement Kalman filtering (CPMKF) method [1]. The statistic property of the converted position measurement errors has been explored in [1–10]. The Doppler or range-rate measurement, which is the only measurement containing target velocity information, is not processed in the CPMKF method.

Due to the high nonlinearity of the Doppler measurement, the filtering process becomes more complex when Doppler is also included as a part of measurement vector. Various nonlinear filtering methods are utilized to handle Doppler measurements [11–18]. The first-order extended Kalman filter (EKF) is used to process the position and Doppler measurements simultaneously [12, 16]. A sequential processing approach, which can not only improve the filtering accuracy but also reduce the computational complexity [19, 20], is used with the first-order EKF [18] to process position and range-rate measurements. Since the EKF is based on a

Taylor series expansion, large errors in the posterior mean and covariance approximation may lead to performance degradations and possible divergence with the highly nonlinear range-rate measurements. The unscented Kalman filter (UKF), which overcomes some of the shortcomings of the EKF based on a deterministic sampling approach, is used to process the Doppler measurements sequentially in [15, 17]. On the other hand, the converted Doppler measurements, constructed by the product of range and Doppler measurement, are used to replace the original Doppler measurement in [13, 14, 21]. Nonlinear recursive filtering methods still have to be employed to extract target information from the nonlinear converted measurements directly, although the nonlinearity is reduced largely [13]. The second-order EKF is utilized to process the converted Doppler measurements and the converted position measurements simultaneously in [21] and sequentially in [13, 14]. The measurement errors amplified by large ranges may result in performance degradation of those converted Doppler measurement-based methods. A linear denoising filter is presented in [22, 23] to reduce the noise contained in the converted Doppler measurement, but only the constant velocity (CV) motion is investigated. In [3], based on the estimated angle cosine and sine, Doppler is treated as an approximate linear function of velocity components to allow the use of linear Kalman filter. Since the angle cosine and sine are all nonlinear functions of target position components, the process is actually nonlinear, and estimation performance may rely on the quality of angle cosine and sine critically.

Although performance improvements have been observed in the existing literature, which use the Doppler measurements in state estimation, performance cannot be guaranteed due to the utilization of nonlinear recursive filtering methods. One of the major advantages of the CPMKF is that the nonlinear approximations (i.e., measurement conversion and statistic evaluation) are performed outside the filtering recursion and nonlinear filters are avoided [24]. Whereas, in the existing nonlinear filtering methods [13, 17, 18], the nonlinear approximation of the Doppler measurements or the converted Doppler measurement is performed inside the dynamic filtering recursion. The accumulations of approximation errors may lead to unsatisfactory performance.

In order to rectify these flaws, a new method is proposed in [27–29] and summarized in this chapter. In the proposed method, the use of nonlinear filtering approaches is also avoided while dealing with the Doppler measurements. First, the pseudo-state vectors, of which the converted Doppler measurements [13, 14, 22, 23] are linear functions, are defined. The pseudo-state vector consists of the converted Doppler (i.e., the product of range and range rate) and its derivatives. The time-evolving equations of the pseudo-states are derived and proven to be linear for the three commonly utilized motion models, the constant velocity (CV), constant turn (CT), and the constant acceleration (CA) models. Then, the converted Doppler measurement Kalman filter (CDMKF), a linear filter, is presented to produce the pseudo-state estimates and filter the noise contained in the converted Doppler measurements. Finally, the CDMKF is carried out along with the CPMKF to establish a new state estimation method, statically fused converted measurement Kalman filters (SF-CMKF). Cartesian state estimates and pseudo-state estimates are provided by CPMKF and CDMKF, respectively, and are then fused by a static estimator to produce final state estimates. The quadratic nonlinearity of the pseudo-states is processed by expanding the pseudo-states up to the second order around the estimates from the CPMKF. The correlation between the CPMKF and CDMKF, caused by the common range measurement and process noise, is involved in the static minimum mean squared error (MMSE) estimator to derive correct fusion of the states from the two linear Kalman filters. This filtering scheme actually converts the dynamic nonlinear estimation problem to a linear dynamic estimation following with a static nonlinear fusion problem, where nonlinearity approximations are carried out outside the filtering recursions and the static fusion part produces estimates only for overall outputting. Therefore, nonlinear filtering is also avoided even when range-rate measurements are used for estimation.

2. Problem formulation

A target's motion is modeled in a two-dimensional (2D) Cartesian system by a discrete time-state equation as

$$\mathbf{X}(k+1) = \mathbf{\Phi}\mathbf{X}(k) + \mathbf{\Gamma}\mathbf{V}(k) \tag{1}$$

where $\mathbf{X}(k)$ is a state vector consisting of position components and corresponding velocity components (or acceleration components) along x and y directions, $\mathbf{\Phi}$ is the state transition matrix, and $\mathbf{\Gamma}$ denotes the noise input matrix.

For CV model,

$$\mathbf{X}(k) = \begin{bmatrix} x(k) \\ \dot{x}(k) \\ y(k) \\ \dot{y}(k) \end{bmatrix}, \mathbf{\Phi} = \begin{bmatrix} 1 & T & 0 & 0 \\ 0 & 1 & 0 & 0 \\ 0 & 0 & 1 & T \\ 0 & 0 & 0 & 1 \end{bmatrix}, \mathbf{\Gamma} = \begin{bmatrix} T^2/2 & 0 \\ T & 0 \\ 0 & T^2/2 \\ 0 & T \end{bmatrix} \tag{2}$$

For CT model,

$$\mathbf{X}(k) = \begin{bmatrix} x(k) \\ \dot{x}(k) \\ y(k) \\ \dot{y}(k) \end{bmatrix}, \mathbf{\Phi} = \begin{bmatrix} 1 & \sin(\varpi T)/\varpi & 0 & (\cos(\varpi T)-1)/\varpi \\ 0 & \cos(\varpi T) & 0 & -\sin(\varpi T) \\ 0 & (1-\cos(\varpi T))/\varpi & 1 & \sin(\varpi T)/\varpi \\ 0 & \sin(\varpi T) & 0 & \cos(\varpi T) \end{bmatrix}, \mathbf{\Gamma} = \begin{bmatrix} T^2/2 & 0 \\ T & 0 \\ 0 & T^2/2 \\ 0 & T \end{bmatrix} \tag{3}$$

For CA model,

$$\mathbf{X}(k) = \begin{bmatrix} x(k) \\ \dot{x}(k) \\ \ddot{x}(k) \\ y(k) \\ \dot{y}(k) \\ \ddot{y}(k) \end{bmatrix}, \mathbf{\Phi} = \begin{bmatrix} 1 & T & T^2/2 & 0 & 0 & 0 \\ 0 & 1 & T & 0 & 0 & 0 \\ 0 & 0 & 1 & 0 & 0 & 0 \\ 0 & 0 & 0 & 1 & T & T^2/2 \\ 0 & 0 & 0 & 0 & 1 & T \\ 0 & 0 & 0 & 0 & 0 & 1 \end{bmatrix}, \mathbf{\Gamma} = \begin{bmatrix} T^2/2 & 0 \\ T & 0 \\ 1 & 0 \\ 0 & T^2/2 \\ 0 & T \\ 0 & 1 \end{bmatrix} \tag{4}$$

where T is the sampling interval. $\mathbf{V}(k) = [v_x(k), v_y(k)]^T$ is the process noise that follows the Gauss distribution with zero mean and known covariance $\mathbf{Q} = \text{diag}[q, q]$. Here, $v_x(k)$ and $v_y(k)$ denote process noises in x and y directions, respectively, and q denotes the process noise intensity. ϖ is the known turn rate for CT model [25].

A 2D Doppler radar is assumed to report measurements of targets in polar coordinates, including range, range rate, and azimuth. The measurement equation can be expressed as

$$\begin{bmatrix} r_m(k) \\ \alpha_m(k) \\ \dot{r}_m(k) \end{bmatrix} = \begin{bmatrix} r(k) \\ \alpha(k) \\ \dot{r}(k) \end{bmatrix} + \begin{bmatrix} \tilde{r}(k) \\ \tilde{\alpha}(k) \\ \tilde{\dot{r}}(k) \end{bmatrix} = \begin{bmatrix} \sqrt{x^2(k)+y^2(k)} \\ \arctan(y(k)/x(k)) \\ (x(k)\dot{x}(k)+y(k)\dot{y}(k))/\sqrt{x^2(k)+y^2(k)} \end{bmatrix} + \begin{bmatrix} \tilde{r}(k) \\ \tilde{\alpha}(k) \\ \tilde{\dot{r}}(k) \end{bmatrix} \quad (5)$$

where $r(k)$, $\alpha(k)$, and $\dot{r}(k)$ are the target's true range, azimuth, and range rate, respectively. $\tilde{r}(k)$, $\tilde{\alpha}(k)$, and $\tilde{\dot{r}}(k)$ are the corresponding measurement noises, which are all assumed to be zero-mean Gaussian noises with known variances σ_r^2, σ_α^2, and $\sigma_{\dot{r}}^2$, respectively. It is assumed that the measurement noises are mutually independent with the exception that $\tilde{r}(k)$ and $\tilde{\dot{r}}(k)$ are statistically correlated [26] with correlation coefficient ρ, i.e., $\text{cov}(\tilde{r}(k), \tilde{\dot{r}}(k)) = \rho\sigma_r\sigma_{\dot{r}}$.

3. Measurement conversion

In this chapter, the CPMKF is utilized to extract information from position (range and azimuth) measurements, and the CDMKF is used to produce pseudo-state estimates from range and range-rate measurements. Fusion of the two converted measurement Kalman filters yields final Cartesian state estimation. For appropriate filtering, the actual statistic, mean and covariance, of the converted measurements has to be evaluated.

The converted position measurements constructed from range and azimuth measurements can be written as

$$\begin{bmatrix} x_c(k) \\ y_c(k) \end{bmatrix} = \begin{bmatrix} r_m(k)\cos\alpha_m(k) \\ r_m(k)\sin\alpha_m(k) \end{bmatrix} = \begin{bmatrix} x(k)+\tilde{x}(k) \\ y(k)+\tilde{y}(k) \end{bmatrix} \quad (6)$$

where $\tilde{x}(k)$ and $\tilde{y}(k)$ are converted measurement errors along x and y directions, respectively. The converted Doppler measurements is constructed by the product of the range and Doppler measurements as

$$\eta_c(k) = r_m(k)\dot{r}_m(k) = \eta(k) + \tilde{\eta}(k) \quad (7)$$

where $\eta(k)$ is the product of true range and range rate, expressed by.

$$\eta(k) = x(k)\dot{x}(k) + y(k)\dot{y}(k) \quad (8)$$

and $\tilde{\eta}(k)$ is the corresponding error. It can be seen from (8), the converted Doppler measurements are nonlinear with respect to Cartesian states. In conventional tracking approaches, which estimate Cartesian states by recursive filtering directly from measurements, nonlinear recursive filters have to be employed, resulting in unsatisfied performance and possible divergence. In this chapter, the converted Doppler measurements are processed first, by a linear filter, to produce pseudo-state estimates, instead of Cartesian state estimates directly.

The converted measurements in (6) are biased [1, 8] due to nonlinear transformations. Both additive [1] and multiplicative [8] debiasing approaches are presented to counter this bias. Some modifications have also been proposed to deal with large errors [4] and correlation between the measurement noise and the covariance [2, 3, 5, 7]. A detailed discussion on the bias issue is beyond the scope of this chapter. In [1], the additive debiasing method is used with converted position measurements. A linearization method based on Taylor series expansion, which may result in large errors, is proposed in [18]. To facilitate a fair comparison against existing works [14, 15] dealing with Doppler measurements, the position measurement conversion is implemented here based on the additive debiasing [1] technique, as in [14, 15].

Using the nested conditioning method [1, 24], which was proven to be effective and consistent, the calculation of the converted Doppler measurement errors was investigated in [14, 15]. The objective of the nested conditioning method is to find the mean and covariance conditioned on the unknown ideal measurement first and then to find their expectations conditioned on the noisy measurement.

Denote the bias and covariance of the converted position measurements as

$$\boldsymbol{\mu}^{p}(k) = [\mu^{x}(k), \mu^{y}(k)]^{T} \tag{9}$$

and

$$\boldsymbol{R}^{p}(k) = \begin{bmatrix} R^{xx}(k) & R^{xy}(k) \\ R^{yx}(k) & R^{yy}(k) \end{bmatrix} \tag{10}$$

respectively. Then the debiased converted position measurements can be obtained as

$$\boldsymbol{Z}_{c}^{p}(k) = \begin{bmatrix} x_{c}(k) \\ y_{c}(k) \end{bmatrix} - \boldsymbol{\mu}^{p}(k) \tag{11}$$

The expressions of the elements in (9) and (10) can be obtained by the nested conditioning method [1] as

$$\mu^{x}(k) = r_{m}(k)\cos\alpha_{m}(k)(e^{-\sigma_{\alpha}^{2}} - e^{-\sigma_{\alpha}^{2}/2}) \tag{12}$$

$$\mu^{y}(k) = r_{m}(k)\sin\alpha_{m}(k)(e^{-\sigma_{\alpha}^{2}} - e^{-\sigma_{\alpha}^{2}/2}) \tag{13}$$

$$\begin{aligned} R^{xx}(k) = {} & r_{m}^{2}(k)e^{-2\sigma_{\alpha}^{2}}\{\cos^{2}\alpha_{m}(k)[\cosh(2\sigma_{\alpha}^{2}) - \cosh(\sigma_{\alpha}^{2})] + \sin^{2}\alpha_{m}(k)[\sinh(2\sigma_{\alpha}^{2}) - \sinh(\sigma_{\alpha}^{2})]\} \\ & + \sigma_{r}^{2}e^{-2\sigma_{\alpha}^{2}}\{\cos^{2}\alpha_{m}(k)[2\cosh(2\sigma_{\alpha}^{2}) - \cosh(\sigma_{\alpha}^{2})] + \sin^{2}\alpha_{m}(k)[2\sinh(2\sigma_{\alpha}^{2}) - \sinh(\sigma_{\alpha}^{2})]\} \end{aligned} \tag{14}$$

$$\begin{aligned} R^{yy}(k) = {} & r_{m}^{2}(k)e^{-2\sigma_{\alpha}^{2}}\{\sin^{2}\alpha_{m}(k)[\cosh(2\sigma_{\alpha}^{2}) - \cosh(\sigma_{\alpha}^{2})] + \cos^{2}\alpha_{m}(k)[\sinh(2\sigma_{\alpha}^{2}) - \sinh(\sigma_{\alpha}^{2})]\} \\ & + \sigma_{r}^{2}e^{-2\sigma_{\alpha}^{2}}\{\sin^{2}\alpha_{m}(k)[2\cosh(2\sigma_{\alpha}^{2}) - \cosh(\sigma_{\alpha}^{2})] + \cos^{2}\alpha_{m}(k)[2\sinh(2\sigma_{\alpha}^{2}) - \sinh(\sigma_{\alpha}^{2})]\} \end{aligned} \tag{15}$$

$$R^{xy}(k) = R^{yx}(k) = \sin\alpha_{m}(k)\cos\alpha_{m}(k)e^{-4\alpha_{\alpha}^{2}}\{\sigma_{r}^{2} + [r_{m}^{2}(k) + \sigma_{r}^{2}](1 - e^{\sigma_{\alpha}^{2}})\} \tag{16}$$

Similarly, one can get the bias and variance of the converted Doppler measurements as [14].

$$\mu^{\eta}(k) = \rho\sigma_{r}\sigma_{\dot{r}} \tag{17}$$

and

$$R^{\eta\eta}(k) = r_{m}^{2}(k)\sigma_{\dot{r}}^{2} + \sigma_{r}^{2}\dot{r}_{m}^{2}(k) + 3(1+\rho^{2})\sigma_{r}^{2}\sigma_{\dot{r}}^{2} + 2r_{m}(k)\dot{r}_{m}(k)\rho\sigma_{r}\sigma_{\dot{r}} \tag{18}$$

respectively. The converted Doppler measurements are debiased as

$$Z_{c}^{\eta}(k) = \eta_{c}(k) - \mu^{\eta}(k) \tag{19}$$

The covariance between the converted position and Doppler measurements is given as

$$\boldsymbol{R}^{p\eta}(k)=\begin{bmatrix}R^{x\eta}(k)\\R^{y\eta}(k)\end{bmatrix}=\begin{bmatrix}[\sigma_r^2\dot{r}_m(k)+r_m(k)\rho\sigma_r\sigma_{\dot{r}}]\cos\alpha_m(k)e^{-\sigma_\alpha^2}\\ [\sigma_r^2\dot{r}_m(k)+r_m(k)\rho\sigma_r\sigma_{\dot{r}}]\sin\alpha_m(k)e^{-\sigma_\alpha^2}\end{bmatrix}\tag{20}$$

For details of the derivations of the measurement errors presented above, see [1, 13, 14].

4. Statically fused converted measurement Kalman filters

The converted position measurements, given by (10) and (11), are preferably processed by the standard linear Kalman filter to outperform practical nonlinear filters (EKF and UKF). The converted Doppler measurements, given by (18) and (19), are also processed by a linear Kalman filter to extract pseudo-state. The outputs of these two linear filters are then fused by a static MMSE estimator to yield the final Cartesian state estimates. This results in the statically fused converted measurement Kalman filter, which is illustrated in **Figure 1**. This method, abbreviated as SF-CMKF, produces superior performance in both accuracy and consistency.

4.1 Pseudo-state equation

Finding the proper representation of a certain motion in the generic state space that corresponds to the converted Doppler is critical to this method. In this section, the pseudo-state equation, consistent with the CV, CA, and CT model in 2D Cartesian state space, is derived first, and then the CDMKF and SF-CMKF filtering procedures are formulated.

4.1.1 Pseudo-state equation for CV model

The CV model in 2D Cartesian coordinates can be described by

$$\begin{bmatrix}\ddot{x}(k)\\\ddot{y}(k)\end{bmatrix}=\begin{bmatrix}0\\0\end{bmatrix}\tag{21}$$

The converted Doppler (8) is considered to be a generic position to define a pseudo-state that is linear with respect to measurement (7). Since the converted Doppler is quadratic in Cartesian states, it has limited derivatives for the CV model. Taking derivatives of the converted Doppler up to the second order using (21), we have

$$\begin{bmatrix}\eta(k)\\\dot{\eta}(k)\\\ddot{\eta}(k)\end{bmatrix}=\begin{bmatrix}x(k)\dot{x}(k)+y(k)\dot{y}(k)\\\dot{x}(k)\dot{x}(k)+y(k)\dot{y}(k)\\0\end{bmatrix}\tag{22}$$

It shows that the CV motion in 2D Cartesian coordinates can be described completely by $\eta(k)$ and its first-order derivative in the state space corresponding to the generic position, converted Doppler. Then the pseudo-state vector can be defined as

$$\boldsymbol{\eta}(k) = \begin{bmatrix} \eta(k) \\ \dot{\eta}(k) \end{bmatrix} = \mathbf{C}[\mathbf{X}(k)] = \begin{bmatrix} x(k)\dot{x}(k) + y(k)\dot{y}(k) \\ \dot{x}(k)\dot{x}(k) + \dot{y}(k)\dot{y}(k) \end{bmatrix} \tag{23}$$

where $\mathbf{C}$ is the vector-valued nonlinear function.

To derive the pseudo-state equation, explicit substitutions are employed. From (23), the pseudo-state at time $k+1$ is given by

$$\boldsymbol{\eta}(k+1) = \begin{bmatrix} \eta(k+1) \\ \dot{\eta}(k+1) \end{bmatrix} = \begin{bmatrix} x(k+1)\dot{x}(k+1) + y(k+1)\dot{y}(k+1) \\ \dot{x}(k+1)\dot{x}(k+1) + \dot{y}(k+1)\dot{y}(k+1) \end{bmatrix} \tag{24}$$

Using (1), (23), and (24), explicit substitutions of the pseudo-state by the Cartesian state equations are performed; the pseudo-state equation can be derived as

$$\boldsymbol{\eta}(k+1) = \boldsymbol{\Phi}_\eta \boldsymbol{\eta}(k) + \mathbf{G}\mathbf{u}(k) + \boldsymbol{\Gamma}_x \mathbf{V}_x(k) + \boldsymbol{\Gamma}_s \mathbf{V}_s(k) \tag{25}$$

where

$$\boldsymbol{\Phi}_\eta = \begin{bmatrix} 1 & T \\ 0 & T \end{bmatrix} \tag{26}$$

$$\mathbf{G} = \boldsymbol{\Gamma}_s = \begin{bmatrix} T^3/2 & T^3/2 \\ T^2 & T^2 \end{bmatrix} \tag{27}$$

$$\mathbf{u}(k) = E\left(\begin{bmatrix} v_x^2(k) \\ v_y^2(k) \end{bmatrix}\right) = \begin{bmatrix} q \\ q \end{bmatrix} \tag{28}$$

$$\boldsymbol{\Gamma}_x = \begin{bmatrix} T & 3T^2/2 \\ 0 & 2T \end{bmatrix} \tag{29}$$

$$\mathbf{V}_x(k) = \mathbf{X}_\Gamma \mathbf{V}(k) = \begin{bmatrix} x(k) & y(k) \\ \dot{x}(k) & \dot{y}(k) \end{bmatrix} \begin{bmatrix} v_x(k) \\ v_y(k) \end{bmatrix} \tag{30}$$

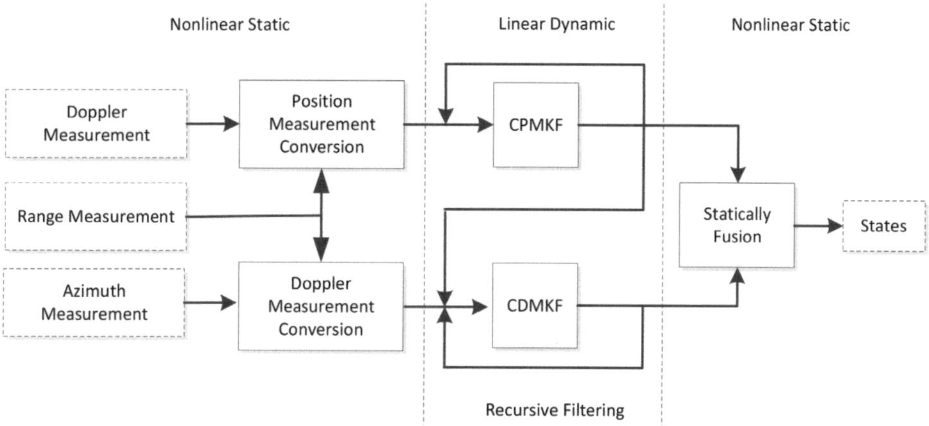

Figure 1.
Filtering structure of SF-CMKF.

$$\mathbf{V}_s(k) = \begin{bmatrix} v_x^2(k) - q \\ v_y^2(k) - q \end{bmatrix} \tag{31}$$

It can be seen from (25)–(31) that the pseudo-states evolve linearly in time, disturbed by the noise part. Based on the assumption that $v_x(k)$, $v_y(k)$, and $v_z(k)$ are white Gaussian with zero mean and mutually independent, we have that the noises $\mathbf{V}_x(k)$ and $\mathbf{V}_s(k)$ are white with zero mean; the corresponding covariance can be obtained as

$$\mathbf{Q}_x(k) = q\left(\begin{bmatrix} x^2(k) & x(k)\dot{x}(k) \\ \dot{x}(k)x(k) & \dot{x}^2(k) \end{bmatrix} + \begin{bmatrix} y^2(k) & y(k)\dot{y}(k) \\ \dot{y}(k)y(k) & \dot{y}^2(k) \end{bmatrix}\right) \tag{32}$$

$$\mathbf{Q}_s(k) = \begin{bmatrix} 2q^2 & 0 \\ 0 & 2q^2 \end{bmatrix} \tag{33}$$

4.1.2 Pseudo-state equation for CA model

Similarly, the pseudo-state equation for CA model can be derived as

$$\boldsymbol{\eta}(k+1) = \boldsymbol{\Phi}_\eta \boldsymbol{\eta}(k) + \mathbf{G}\mathbf{u}(k) + \boldsymbol{\Gamma}_x \mathbf{V}_x(k) + \boldsymbol{\Gamma}_s \mathbf{V}_s(k) \tag{34}$$

where

$$\boldsymbol{\eta}(k) = \begin{bmatrix} \eta(k) \\ \dot{\eta}(k) \\ \ddot{\eta}(k) \\ \dddot{\eta}(k) \end{bmatrix} = \mathbf{C}[\mathrm{X}(k)] = \begin{bmatrix} x(k)\dot{x}(k) + y(k)\dot{y}(k) \\ \dot{x}(k)\dot{x}(k) + \dot{y}(k)\dot{y}(k) + x(k)\ddot{x}(k) + y(k)\ddot{y}(k) \\ 3\dot{x}(k)\ddot{x}(k) + 3\dot{y}(k)\ddot{y}(k) \\ 3\ddot{x}^2(k) + 3\ddot{y}^2(k) \end{bmatrix} \tag{35}$$

$$\boldsymbol{\Phi}_\eta = \begin{bmatrix} 1 & T & T^2/2 & T^3/6 \\ 0 & 1 & T & T^2/2 \\ 0 & 0 & 1 & T \\ 0 & 0 & 0 & 1 \end{bmatrix} \tag{36}$$

$$\mathbf{G} = \boldsymbol{\Gamma}_s = \begin{bmatrix} T^3/2 & T^3/2 \\ 3T^2/2 & 3T^2/2 \\ 3T & 3T \\ 3 & 3 \end{bmatrix} \tag{37}$$

$$\mathbf{u}(k) = E\left(\begin{bmatrix} v_x^2(k) \\ v_y^2(k) \end{bmatrix}\right) = \begin{bmatrix} q \\ q \end{bmatrix} \tag{38}$$

$$\boldsymbol{\Gamma}_x = \begin{bmatrix} T & 3T^2/2 & T^3 \\ 1 & 3T & 3T^2 \\ 0 & 3 & 6T \\ 0 & 0 & 6 \end{bmatrix} \tag{39}$$

$$\mathbf{V}_x(k) = \mathbf{X}_\Gamma \mathbf{V}(k) = \begin{bmatrix} x(k) & y(k) \\ \dot{x}(k) & \dot{y}(k) \\ \ddot{x}(k) & \ddot{y}(k) \end{bmatrix} \begin{bmatrix} v_x(k) \\ v_y(k) \end{bmatrix} \tag{40}$$

$$\mathbf{V}_s(k)=\begin{bmatrix} v_x^2(k)-q \\ v_y^2(k)-q \end{bmatrix} \tag{41}$$

The noises $\mathbf{V}_x(k)$ and $\mathbf{V}_s(k)$ are white with zero mean; the corresponding covariance can be obtained as

$$\mathbf{Q}_x(k)=q\left(\begin{bmatrix} x^2(k) & x(k)\dot{x}(k) & x(k)\ddot{x}(k) \\ \dot{x}(k)x(k) & \dot{x}^2(k) & \dot{x}(k)\ddot{x}(k) \\ \ddot{x}(k)x(k) & \ddot{x}(k)\dot{x}(k) & \ddot{x}^2(k) \end{bmatrix}+\begin{bmatrix} y^2(k) & y(k)\dot{y}(k) & y(k)\ddot{y}(k) \\ \dot{y}(k)y(k) & \dot{y}^2(k) & \dot{y}(k)\ddot{y}(k) \\ \ddot{y}(k)y(k) & \ddot{y}(k)\dot{y}(k) & \ddot{y}^2(k) \end{bmatrix}\right) \tag{42}$$

$$\mathbf{Q}_s(k)=\begin{bmatrix} 2q^2 & 0 \\ 0 & 2q^2 \end{bmatrix} \tag{43}$$

4.1.3 Pseudo-state equation for CT model

Similarly, the pseudo-state equation for CT model can be derived as

$$\boldsymbol{\eta}(k+1)=\boldsymbol{\Phi}_\eta\boldsymbol{\eta}(k)+\mathbf{G}\mathbf{u}(k)+\boldsymbol{\Gamma}_x\mathbf{V}_x(k)+\boldsymbol{\Gamma}_s\mathbf{V}_s(k) \tag{44}$$

where

$$\boldsymbol{\eta}(k)=\begin{bmatrix} \eta(k) \\ \dot{\eta}(k) \end{bmatrix}=\mathrm{C}[\mathrm{X}(k)]=\begin{bmatrix} x(k)\dot{x}(k)+y(k)\dot{y}(k) \\ \dot{x}(k)\dot{x}(k)+y(k)\dot{y}(k)+\varpi(\dot{x}(k)y(k)-x(k)\dot{y}(k)) \end{bmatrix} \tag{45}$$

$$\boldsymbol{\Phi}_\eta=\begin{bmatrix} \cos(\varpi T) & \sin(\varpi T)/\varpi \\ -\varpi\sin(\varpi T) & \cos(\varpi T) \end{bmatrix} \tag{46}$$

$$\mathbf{G}=\boldsymbol{\Gamma}_s=\begin{bmatrix} T^3/2 & T^3/2 \\ T^2 & T^2 \end{bmatrix} \tag{47}$$

$$\mathbf{u}(k)=E\left(\begin{bmatrix} v_x^2(k) \\ v_y^2(k) \end{bmatrix}\right)=\begin{bmatrix} q \\ q \end{bmatrix} \tag{48}$$

$$\boldsymbol{\Gamma}_x=\begin{bmatrix} 1 & 0 \\ 0 & 1 \end{bmatrix} \tag{49}$$

$$\mathbf{V}_x(k)=\mathbf{X}_\Gamma\mathbf{V}(k)=\begin{bmatrix} A & B \\ C & D \end{bmatrix}\begin{bmatrix} v_x(k) \\ v_y(k) \end{bmatrix} \tag{50}$$

$$\mathbf{V}_s(k)=\begin{bmatrix} v_x^2(k)-q \\ v_y^2(k)-q \end{bmatrix} \tag{51}$$

In the above

$$A=Tx(k+1|k)+T^2\dot{x}(k+1|k)/2 \tag{52}$$

$$B=Ty(k+1|k)+T^2\dot{y}(k+1|k)/2 \tag{53}$$

$$C=T(\varpi y(k+1|k)+2\dot{x}(k+1|k))-T^2\varpi\dot{y}(k+1|k)/2 \tag{54}$$

$$D=T(-\varpi x(k+1|k)+2\dot{y}(k+1|k))+T^2\varpi\dot{x}(k+1|k)/2 \tag{55}$$

where

$$x(k+1|k) = x(k) + \sin(\varpi T)\dot{x}(k)/\varpi - (1-\cos(\varpi T))\dot{y}(k)/\varpi \tag{56}$$

$$\dot{x}(k+1|k) = \cos(\varpi T)\dot{x}(k) - \sin(\varpi T)\dot{y}(k) \tag{57}$$

$$y(k+1|k) = y(k) + \sin(\varpi T)\dot{y}(k)/\varpi + (1-\cos(\varpi T))\dot{x}(k)/\varpi \tag{58}$$

$$\dot{y}(k+1|k) = \sin(\varpi T)\dot{x}(k) + \cos(\varpi T)\dot{y}(k) \tag{59}$$

The noises $\mathbf{V}_x(k)$ and $\mathbf{V}_s(k)$ are white with zero mean; the corresponding covariance can be obtained as

$$\mathbf{Q}_x(k) = \mathbf{X}_\Gamma \begin{bmatrix} q & 0 \\ 0 & q \end{bmatrix} \mathbf{X}_\Gamma^T \tag{60}$$

$$\mathbf{Q}_s(k) = \begin{bmatrix} 2q^2 & 0 \\ 0 & 2q^2 \end{bmatrix} \tag{61}$$

For CV, CA, and CT models, the cross-covariance between $\mathbf{V}_s(k)$ and $\mathbf{V}_x(k)$ is proven to be zero. Therefore, the disturbance part in the pseudo-state equation can be treated as white. Additionally, the pseudo-state equation can be considered as linear. In this case, the MMSE can be used to produce a best linear estimation.

4.2 Converted doppler measurement Kalman filter

The debiased converted Doppler measurements $Z_c^\eta(k)$ in (19) guarantee the observability of the pseudo-states in (23), (25), (34), (35), (44), and (45) with the measurement matrix given as $\mathbf{H}_\eta = \begin{bmatrix} 1 & \mathbf{0}_{1*n_\eta} \end{bmatrix}$, where n_η is the dimension of the pseudo-state. The measurement equation is given by

$$Z_c^\eta(k) = \mathbf{H}_\eta \boldsymbol{\eta}(k) + W_\eta(k) \tag{62}$$

In the above, $W_\eta(k)$ denotes the zero-mean Gaussian measurement noise with known variance given by (18). The CDMKF is derived under the linear minimum mean squared error (LMMSE) estimation frameworks as follows:

Applying the expectation operator on the pseudo-state (25), (34), and (44) conditioned on the converted Doppler measurements up to time step k, we can obtain the predicted pseudo-state as

$$\hat{\boldsymbol{\eta}}(k+1,k) = \boldsymbol{\Phi}_\eta \hat{\boldsymbol{\eta}}(k,k) + \mathbf{G}\mathbf{u}(k) \tag{63}$$

Subtracting the above from the pseudo-state equation yields the state prediction error

$$\tilde{\boldsymbol{\eta}}(k+1,k) = \boldsymbol{\eta}(k+1) - \hat{\boldsymbol{\eta}}(k+1,k) = \boldsymbol{\Phi}_\eta \tilde{\boldsymbol{\eta}}(k,k) + \boldsymbol{\Gamma}_x \mathbf{V}_x(k) + \boldsymbol{\Gamma}_s \mathbf{V}_s(k) \tag{64}$$

where $\tilde{\eta}(k,k)$ is the estimation error at time step k. Then the state prediction covariance is

$$\mathbf{P}_\eta(k+1,k) = E[\tilde{\boldsymbol{\eta}}(k+1,k)\tilde{\boldsymbol{\eta}}^T(k+1,k)] = \boldsymbol{\Phi}_\eta \mathbf{P}_\eta(k,k)\boldsymbol{\Phi}_\eta^T + \boldsymbol{\Gamma}_x \mathbf{Q}_x(k)\boldsymbol{\Gamma}_x^T + \boldsymbol{\Gamma}_s \mathbf{Q}_s(k)\boldsymbol{\Gamma}_s^T \tag{65}$$

The predicted measurement can be obtained similarly by taking expectation (62) conditioned on the measurements until time step $k$as

$$\hat{Z}_c^{\eta}(k+1,k) = \mathbf{H}_{\eta}\hat{\boldsymbol{\eta}}(k+1,k) \tag{66}$$

Subtracting the above from (62), the measurement prediction error can be written as

$$\tilde{Z}_c^{\eta}(k+1,k) = \mathbf{H}_{\eta}\tilde{\boldsymbol{\eta}}(k+1,k) + W_{\eta}(k) \tag{67}$$

Then the measurement prediction covariance is given by

$$\mathbf{S}_{\eta}(k+1) = E[\tilde{Z}_c^{\eta}(k+1,k)\tilde{Z}_c^{\eta}(k+1,k)^T] = \mathbf{H}_{\eta}\mathbf{P}_{\eta}(k+1,k)\mathbf{H}_{\eta}^T + R^{\eta\eta}(k) \tag{68}$$

And the cross-covariance between the pseudo-state and the measurement is

$$\mathbf{P}_{\eta z}(k+1,k) = E[\tilde{\boldsymbol{\eta}}(k+1,k)\tilde{Z}_c^{\eta}(k+1,k)^T] = \mathbf{P}_{\eta}(k+1,k)\mathbf{H}_{\eta}^T \tag{69}$$

The filter gain is calculated by

$$\mathbf{K}_{\eta}(k+1) = \mathbf{P}_{\eta z}(k+1,k)\mathbf{S}_{\eta}^{-1}(k+1) = \mathbf{P}_{\eta}(k+1,k)\mathbf{H}_{\eta}^T\mathbf{S}_{\eta}^{-1}(k+1) \tag{70}$$

Then the updated pseudo-state at time step k is given as

$$\hat{\boldsymbol{\eta}}(k+1,k+1) = \hat{\boldsymbol{\eta}}(k+1,k) + \mathbf{K}_{\eta}(k+1)[Z_c^{\eta}(k) - \hat{Z}_c^{\eta}(k+1,k)] \tag{71}$$

And the updated covariance is

$$\mathbf{P}_{\eta}(k+1,k+1) = \mathbf{P}_{\eta}(k+1,k) - \mathbf{P}_{\eta z}(k+1,k)\mathbf{S}_{\eta}^{-1}(k+1)\mathbf{P}_{\eta z}^T(k+1,k) \tag{72}$$

Eqs. (63)–(72) summarize the filtering procedure of the CDMKF with the key matrix parameters defined by the pseudo-state equation. The whiteness of the process noise and the linearity of the state equations guarantee that the CDMKF is a best linear estimator in the sense of MMSE. This provides a new method, rather than a nonlinear filter, to mitigate the noises in Doppler measurements and extract target information in pseudo-state space.

Note that the Cartesian state at time k is required to determine the matrix X_{Γ} in (30), (40), and (50). In practice, the true state is not available. The solution is to replace the true state by the state estimates $[\hat{\mathbf{X}}_p(k,k), \mathbf{P}_p(k,k)]$ at time step k from the CPMKF. Also, the covariance $\mathbf{Q}_x(k)$ for CV model in (32) can be approximated using components of $[\hat{\mathbf{X}}_p(k,k), \mathbf{P}_p(k,k)]$ as

$$\begin{aligned}\mathbf{Q}_x(k) = q&\left(\begin{bmatrix} \hat{x}^2(k) & \hat{x}(k)\hat{\dot{x}}(k) \\ \hat{\dot{x}}(k)\hat{x}(k) & \hat{\dot{x}}^2(k) \end{bmatrix} + \begin{bmatrix} \hat{y}^2(k) & \hat{y}(k)\hat{\dot{y}}(k) \\ \hat{\dot{y}}(k)\hat{y}(k) & \hat{\dot{y}}^2(k) \end{bmatrix}\right) \\ &-q\left(\begin{bmatrix} P^{xx}(k) & P^{x\dot{x}}(k) \\ P^{\dot{x}x}(k) & P^{\dot{x}\dot{x}}(k) \end{bmatrix} + \begin{bmatrix} P^{yy}(k) & P^{y\dot{y}}(k) \\ P^{\dot{y}y}(k) & P^{\dot{y}\dot{y}}(k) \end{bmatrix}\right)\end{aligned} \tag{73}$$

and the covariance $\mathbf{Q}_x(k)$ for CA model in (42) can be approximated as

$$\mathbf{Q}_x(k) = q\left(\begin{bmatrix} \hat{x}^2(k) & \hat{x}(k)\hat{\dot{x}}(k) & \hat{x}(k)\hat{\ddot{x}}(k) \\ \hat{\dot{x}}(k)\hat{x}(k) & \hat{\dot{x}}^2(k) & \hat{\dot{x}}(k)\hat{\ddot{x}}(k) \\ \hat{\ddot{x}}(k)\hat{x}(k) & \hat{\ddot{x}}(k)\hat{\dot{x}}(k) & \hat{\ddot{x}}^2(k) \end{bmatrix} + \begin{bmatrix} \hat{y}^2(k) & \hat{y}(k)\hat{\dot{y}}(k) & \hat{y}(k)\hat{\ddot{y}}(k) \\ \hat{\dot{y}}(k)\hat{y}(k) & \hat{\dot{y}}^2(k) & \hat{\dot{y}}(k)\hat{\ddot{y}}(k) \\ \hat{\ddot{y}}(k)\hat{y}(k) & \hat{\ddot{y}}(k)\hat{\dot{y}}(k) & \hat{\ddot{y}}^2(k) \end{bmatrix}\right)$$
$$- q\left(\begin{bmatrix} P^{xx}(k) & P^{x\dot{x}}(k) & P^{x\ddot{x}}(k) \\ P^{\dot{x}x}(k) & P^{\dot{x}\dot{x}}(k) & P^{\dot{x}\ddot{x}}(k) \\ P^{\ddot{x}x}(k) & P^{\ddot{x}\dot{x}}(k) & P^{\ddot{x}\ddot{x}}(k) \end{bmatrix} + \begin{bmatrix} P^{yy}(k) & P^{y\dot{y}}(k) & P^{y\ddot{y}}(k) \\ P^{\dot{y}y}(k) & P^{\dot{y}\dot{y}}(k) & P^{\dot{y}\ddot{y}}(k) \\ P^{\ddot{y}y}(k) & P^{\ddot{y}\dot{y}}(k) & P^{\ddot{y}\ddot{y}}(k) \end{bmatrix}\right) \tag{74}$$

4.3 Converted position measurement Kalman filter

The formulations of the CPMKF are also given for derivation of the SF-CMKF. The state equation and measurement equation can be expressed as

$$\mathbf{X}_p(k+1) = \mathbf{\Phi}_p(k)\mathbf{X}_p(k) + \mathbf{\Gamma}_p\mathbf{V}(k) \tag{75}$$

$$\boldsymbol{Z}_c^P(k) = \mathbf{H}_p(k)\mathbf{X}_p(k) + \mathbf{W}_p(k) \tag{76}$$

The process noise $\mathbf{V}(k)$ is identical to those in (30), (40), and (50). Here, $\boldsymbol{Z}_c^P(k)$ is the debiased converted position measurement in (11). The converted measurement error $\mathbf{W}_p(k)$ is zero mean with known covariance in (10). The subscript p is utilized to indicate the matrixes or variables are related to the CPMKF. The implementation procedure of CPMKF is as below:

$$\hat{\mathbf{X}}_p(k+1,k) = \mathbf{\Phi}_p\hat{\mathbf{X}}_p(k,k) \tag{77}$$

$$\mathbf{P}_p(k+1,k) = \mathbf{\Phi}_p\mathbf{P}_p(k,k)\mathbf{\Phi}_p^T + \mathbf{Q}(k) \tag{78}$$

$$\mathbf{K}_p(k+1) = \mathbf{P}_p(k+1,k)\mathbf{H}_p^T[\mathbf{H}_p\mathbf{P}_p(k+1,k)\mathbf{H}_p^T + \mathbf{R}^P(k+1)]^{-1} \tag{79}$$

$$\hat{\mathbf{X}}_p(k+1,k+1) = \hat{\mathbf{X}}_p(k+1,k) + \mathbf{K}_p(k+1)[\boldsymbol{Z}_c^P(k+1) - \mathbf{H}_p\hat{\mathbf{X}}_p(k+1,k)] \tag{80}$$

$$\mathbf{P}_p(k+1,k+1) = \mathbf{P}_p(k+1,k) - \mathbf{K}_p(k+1)\mathbf{H}_p\mathbf{P}_p(k+1,k) \tag{81}$$

4.4 Correlation between CDMKF and CPMKF

As shown in **Figure 1**, the range measurements are commonly used in CDMKF and CPMKF. Therefore, the pseudo-state produced by the CDMKF and the Cartesian states from the CPMKF are not independent. The correlation should be handled appropriately in the fusion procedure.

According to the formulations in the CDMKF, we can rewrite the state estimate from CDMKF at time step $k+1$ as

$$\hat{\boldsymbol{\eta}}(k+1,k+1) = \mathbf{\Phi}_\eta\hat{\boldsymbol{\eta}}(k,k) + \mathbf{Gu}(k) + \mathbf{K}_\eta(k+1)[Z_c^\eta(k+1) - \mathbf{H}_\eta\Phi_\eta\hat{\boldsymbol{\eta}}(k,k) - \mathbf{H}_\eta\mathbf{Gu}(k)] \tag{82}$$

Then the corresponding estimation error is

$$\begin{aligned} &\tilde{\boldsymbol{\eta}}(k+1,k+1) = \boldsymbol{\eta}(k+1) - \hat{\boldsymbol{\eta}}(k+1,k+1) \\ &= [\mathbf{\Phi}_\eta\hat{\boldsymbol{\eta}}(k) + \mathbf{Gu}(k) + \mathbf{\Gamma}_x\mathbf{V}_x(k) + \mathbf{\Gamma}_s\mathbf{V}_s(k)] - [\mathbf{\Phi}_\eta\hat{\boldsymbol{\eta}}(k,k) + \mathbf{Gu}(k)] \\ &\text{-}\mathbf{K}_\eta(k+1)\{\mathbf{H}_\eta[\mathbf{\Phi}_\eta\hat{\boldsymbol{\eta}}(k) + \mathbf{Gu}(k) + \mathbf{\Gamma}_x\mathbf{V}_x(k) + \mathbf{\Gamma}_s\mathbf{V}_s(k)] + W_\eta(k+1) - \mathbf{H}_\eta[\mathbf{\Phi}_\eta\hat{\boldsymbol{\eta}}(k,k) + \mathbf{Gu}(k)]\} \\ &= [\mathbf{I} - \mathbf{K}_\eta(k+1)\mathbf{H}_\eta]\mathbf{\Phi}_\eta\tilde{\boldsymbol{\eta}}(k,k) + [\mathbf{I} - \mathbf{K}_\eta(k+1)\mathbf{H}_\eta]\mathbf{\Gamma}_x\mathbf{V}_x(k) \\ &+[\mathbf{I} - \mathbf{K}_\eta(k+1)\mathrm{H}_\eta]\mathbf{\Gamma}_s\mathbf{V}_s(k) - \mathbf{K}_\eta(k+1)W_\eta(k+1) \end{aligned} \tag{83}$$

Similarly, the filtering error of CPMKF at time $k+1$ step can be obtained as

$$\begin{aligned}\tilde{\mathbf{X}}_p(k+1,k+1) &= \mathbf{X}_p(k+1) - \hat{\mathbf{X}}_p(k+1,k+1)\\ &= [\mathbf{I}-\mathbf{K}_p(k+1)\mathbf{H}_p]\boldsymbol{\Phi}_p\tilde{\mathbf{X}}_p(k,k) + [\mathbf{I}-\mathbf{K}_p(k+1)\mathbf{H}_p]\boldsymbol{\Gamma}_p\mathbf{V}_p(k) - \mathbf{K}_p(k+1)\mathbf{W}_p(k+1)\end{aligned} \tag{84}$$

Multiplying (84) by the transpose of (83) and taking expectation, the covariance between the parallel two filters can be updated recursively as

$$\begin{aligned}\mathbf{P}_{p\eta}(k+1,k+1) &= E[\tilde{\mathbf{X}}_p(k+1,k+1)\tilde{\boldsymbol{\eta}}^T(k+1,k+1)]\\ &= [\mathbf{I}-\mathbf{K}_p(k+1)\mathbf{H}_p]\boldsymbol{\Phi}_p\mathbf{P}_{p\eta}(k,k)\boldsymbol{\Phi}_\eta^T[\mathbf{I}-\mathbf{K}_\eta(k+1)\mathbf{H}_\eta]^T\\ &\quad + [\mathbf{I}-\mathbf{K}_p(k+1)\mathbf{H}_p]\boldsymbol{\Gamma}_p\mathbf{Q}(k)(\boldsymbol{\Gamma}_x\mathbf{X}_\Gamma)^T[\mathbf{I}-\mathbf{K}_\eta(k+1)\mathbf{H}_\eta]^T\\ &\quad + \mathbf{K}_p(k+1)R^{p\eta}(k+1)\mathbf{K}_\eta^T(k+1)\end{aligned} \tag{85}$$

In the above, $R^{p\eta}(k+1)$ is the cross-covariance between the converted position and Doppler measurements at time step $k+1$. It can be given by (20). The above equation is a Lyapunov-type equation. The initial condition can be obtained from the initial covariance between the converted measurements.

4.5 Static fusion of CDMKF and CPMKF

The challenges, when combing the estimates from the CDMKF and CPMKF to obtain final state estimates, are not only the nonlinearity but also the correlation between the CDMKF and CPMKF. Since the pseudo-states from the CDMKF are quadratic in Cartesian states, the nonlinearity can be dealt with by expanding the pseudo-states up to the second order in a Taylor series. In the meantime, the cross-covariance between these two filters should also be taken into account. A static estimator is derived based on the framework of linear MMSE estimator to fuse the outputs from the two filters, with both the nonlinearity and the dependence handled simultaneously.

The problem is to estimate target states at time step $k+1$ using the pseudo-state estimates $\hat{\boldsymbol{\eta}}(k+1,k+1)$ produced by the CDMKF and the Cartesian state estimates $\hat{\mathbf{X}}_p(k+1,k+1)$ from the CPMKF. The prior mean of the state is

$$\bar{\mathbf{X}}(k+1) \rightarrow \hat{\mathbf{X}}_p(k+1,k+1) = E[\mathbf{X}(k+1) \mid \hat{\mathbf{X}}_p(k+1,k+1)] \tag{86}$$

given the state estimates of the CPMKF.

A "measurement"

$$\boldsymbol{Z}(k+1) \rightarrow \hat{\boldsymbol{\eta}}(k+1,k+1) = \boldsymbol{\eta}(k+1) - \tilde{\boldsymbol{\eta}}(k+1,k+1) \tag{87}$$

is constructed to update the state of interest. The error $\tilde{\boldsymbol{\eta}}(k+1,k+1)$ is assumed zero mean, with known covariance $\mathbf{P}_\eta(k+1,k+1)$, and is correlated to the estimation error of the CPMKF

$$\tilde{\mathbf{X}}_p(k+1,k+1) = \mathbf{X}(k+1) - \hat{\mathbf{X}}_p(k+1,k+1) \tag{88}$$

with cross-covariance $\mathrm{P}_{p\eta}(k+1,k+1)$ in (85).

To obtain the prior mean of measurement $\boldsymbol{Z}(k+1)$, the nonlinear function $\mathbf{C}$ between pseudo-states from CDMKF and Cartesian states is expanded as a Taylor series around $\hat{\mathbf{X}}_p(k+1,k+1)$ with terms up to the second order as

$$
\begin{aligned}
Z &= \hat{\boldsymbol{\eta}} = \boldsymbol{\eta} - \tilde{\boldsymbol{\eta}} = \mathbf{C}(\mathbf{X}) - \tilde{\boldsymbol{\eta}} \\
&= \mathbf{C}(\hat{\mathbf{X}}_p) + \dot{\mathbf{C}}(\mathbf{X} - \hat{\mathbf{X}}_p) + \frac{1}{2}\sum_{i=1}^{n_\eta} \mathbf{e}_i (\mathbf{X} - \hat{\mathbf{X}}_p)^T \ddot{\mathbf{C}}(\mathbf{X} - \hat{\mathbf{X}}_p) + HOT - \tilde{\boldsymbol{\eta}}
\end{aligned} \tag{89}
$$

Since the calculations are all performed at a single time step $k+1$, the time subscript is omitted for simplicity. Here, $\mathbf{e}_i$ denotes the ith n_η Cartesian basis vector.

In the above,

$$
\dot{\mathbf{C}} = [\nabla_{\mathbf{x}} \mathbf{C}(\mathbf{X})^T]^T \Big|_{\mathbf{x}=\hat{\mathbf{x}}_p(k+1,k+1)} = \frac{\partial \mathbf{C}}{\partial \mathbf{X}} \tag{90}
$$

is the Jacobian of the vector $\mathbf{C}$, evaluated at $\hat{\mathbf{X}}_p(k+1,k+1)$. Also,

$$
\ddot{\mathbf{C}}^i = [\nabla_{\mathbf{x}} \nabla_{\mathbf{x}}^T \mathbf{C}^i(\mathbf{X})] \Big|_{\mathbf{x}=\hat{\mathbf{x}}_p(k+1,k+1)} = \frac{\partial^2 \mathbf{C}^i}{\partial \mathbf{X}^2} \tag{91}
$$

is the Hessian of the ith component of $\mathbf{C}$, and HOT stands for the higher-order terms, which are all zero for the components with quadratic nonlinearity.

The prior mean of the measurement can be obtained by taking expectation on (89) conditioned on the estimates from the CPMKF as

$$
\bar{Z}(k+1) = \bar{\boldsymbol{\eta}}(k+1) = \mathbf{C}(\hat{\mathbf{X}}_p) + \frac{1}{2}\sum_{i=1}^{n_\eta} \mathbf{e}_i tr(\ddot{\mathbf{C}}^i \mathbf{P}_p) \tag{92}
$$

Then the covariance between the states to be estimated and the "measurement" is, incorporating their dependence,

$$
\begin{aligned}
\mathbf{P}_{\mathbf{xz}} &= E[(\mathbf{X} - \bar{\mathbf{X}})(Z - \bar{Z})^T] \\
&= E\{(\mathbf{X} - \hat{\mathbf{X}}_p)[\dot{\mathbf{C}}(\mathbf{X} - \hat{\mathbf{X}}_p) + \frac{1}{2}\sum_{i=1}^{n_\eta} \mathbf{e}_i ((\mathbf{X} - \hat{\mathbf{X}}_p)^T \ddot{\mathbf{C}}^i (\mathbf{X} - \hat{\mathbf{X}}_p) - tr(\ddot{\mathbf{C}}^i \mathbf{P}_p)) - \tilde{\boldsymbol{\eta}}]^T\} \\
&= \mathbf{P}_p \dot{\mathbf{C}}^T - \mathbf{P}_{p\eta}
\end{aligned} \tag{93}
$$

The covariance of the measurement is

$$
\begin{aligned}
\mathbf{P}_{\mathbf{zz}} &= E[(Z - \bar{Z})(Z - \bar{Z})^T] \\
&= \dot{\mathbf{C}}\mathbf{P}_p \dot{\mathbf{C}}^T + \mathbf{P}_\eta + \frac{1}{2}\sum_{i=1}^{n_\eta}\sum_{j=1}^{n_\eta} \mathbf{e}_i \mathbf{e}_j^T tr(\ddot{\mathbf{C}}^i \mathbf{P}_p \ddot{\mathbf{C}}^j \mathbf{P}_p) - \dot{\mathbf{C}}\mathbf{P}_{p\eta} - (\dot{\mathbf{C}}\mathbf{P}_{p\eta})^T
\end{aligned} \tag{94}
$$

The items with $\mathbf{P}_{p\eta}$ in (93) and (94) arise from the correlation between the two converted measurement filters, and the other items are the same as the measurement update of the second-order EKF.

The static nonlinear estimates are obtained as

$$
\hat{\mathbf{X}} = \hat{\mathbf{X}}_p + \mathbf{P}_{\mathbf{xz}}(\mathbf{P}_{\mathbf{zz}})^{-1}(\hat{\boldsymbol{\eta}} - \bar{Z}) \tag{95}
$$

The covariance associated with this combined estimate is

$$
\mathbf{P} = \mathbf{P}_p - \mathbf{P}_{\mathbf{xz}}(\mathbf{P}_{\mathbf{zz}})^{-1}(\mathbf{P}_{\mathbf{xz}})^T \tag{96}
$$

The final target states are then evaluated by (95) from the pseudo-state estimates of the CDMKF and the state estimates of the CPMKF.

4.6 Initialization

In the SF-CMKF, there are three estimators that need to be initialized: (1) the CPMKF, (2) the CDMKF, and (3) the static fuser.

The two-point differencing method, which uses measurements from two consecutive time steps $\boldsymbol{Z}(k-1)$ and $\boldsymbol{Z}(k)$ to estimate the n_s "position" components $\dot{\mathbf{s}}_I(k)$ and the corresponding "velocity" components $\mathbf{s}_I(k)$ and the measurement covariance $\boldsymbol{R}(k)$ to approximate state covariance $\mathbf{P}(k)$, is used. The initial state has the form as

$$\mathbf{x}_I(k) = \begin{bmatrix} \mathbf{s}_I(k) \\ \dot{\mathbf{s}}_I(k) \\ \mathbf{0}_{n_a \times 1} \end{bmatrix} = \begin{bmatrix} \boldsymbol{Z}(k) \\ [\boldsymbol{Z}(k) - \boldsymbol{Z}(k-1)]/T \\ \mathbf{0}_{n_a \times 1} \end{bmatrix} \quad (97)$$

where $\mathbf{0}_{n_a \times 1}$ is the remaining n_a components. The corresponding covariance is given by

$$\mathbf{P}(k) = \begin{bmatrix} \boldsymbol{R}(k) & \boldsymbol{R}(k)/T & \mathbf{0}_{n_a \times n_s} \\ \boldsymbol{R}(k)/T & 2\boldsymbol{R}(k)/T^2 & \mathbf{0}_{n_a \times n_s} \\ \mathbf{0}_{n_s \times n_a} & \mathbf{0}_{n_s \times n_a} & \mathbf{A}_{n_a \times n_a} \end{bmatrix} \quad (98)$$

$$\mathbf{A}_{n_a \times n_a} = diag(\langle \mathbf{a}_{\max}, \mathbf{a}_{\max} \rangle / 4) \quad (99)$$

where $\mathbf{a}_{\max}$ is the vector consisting of maximum values of the remaining n_a components.

The initialization of the three estimators can be implemented all based on (97) and (98), using correct measurements and measurement covariance.

To initialize the CPMKF, we should use the converted position measurements in (11) and the converted position measurement covariance in (10). To initialize the CDMKF, the converted Doppler measurements in (19) and the corresponding covariance in (18) are used to calculate (97) and (98).

The initialization of the static estimator in the fusion step can be implemented similarly to (98) as

$$\mathbf{P}_{p\eta}(k) = \begin{bmatrix} \boldsymbol{R}^{p\eta}(k) & \boldsymbol{R}^{p\eta}(k)/T & \mathbf{0}_{n_a \times n_s} \\ \boldsymbol{R}^{p\eta}(k)/T & 2\boldsymbol{R}^{p\eta}(k)/T^2 & \mathbf{0}_{n_a \times n_s} \\ \mathbf{0}_{n_s \times n_a} & \mathbf{0}_{n_s \times n_a} & \mathbf{0}_{n_a \times n_a} \end{bmatrix} \quad (100)$$

where $\boldsymbol{R}^{p\eta}(k)$ is the cross-covariance (20) between the converted position measurements and the converted Doppler measurements. Here, matrix $\mathbf{A}_{n_a \times n_a}$ is replaced by $\mathbf{0}_{n_a \times n_a}$, which is because there is no correlation between the states that are initialized to zero.

5. Conclusions

Tracking with position and Doppler measurements, where the range and Doppler measurement errors may be correlated, was considered in this chapter.

First, the converted Doppler measurement Kalman filter, a linear filtering approach, can be used to improve state estimation results with the converted

Doppler measurements, which are constructed by the product of the range and Doppler measurements. This estimation produces pseudo-state estimate. The pseudo-state equations for three commonly used target motion models, the CV, CA, and CT models, were presented, and the filtering procedures were derived.

Based on the converted Doppler measurement Kalman filter and the converted position measurement Kalman filter, a novel tracking filter was proposed to estimate target states from position and Doppler measurements. In this approach, the two converted measurement Kalman filters are used to produce recursive state estimates individually, and their outputs are fused outside the filtering recursion by a static nonlinear estimator, with nonlinearity and correlation handled properly. Since nonlinear operations are all shifted outside the filtering recursions and the two dynamic filters are the best linear MMSE estimators, the proposed method mitigates the effects of nonlinear filtering methods.

Author details

Gongjian Zhou* and Zhengkun Guo
Harbin Institute of Technology, Harbin, China

*Address all correspondence to: zhougj@hit.edu.cn

References

[1] Lerro D, Bar-Shalom Y. Tracking with debiased consistent converted measurements versus EKF. IEEE Transactions on Aerospace and Electronic Systems. 1993;**29**(3): 1015-1022. DOI: 10.1109/7.220948

[2] Bordonaro SV, Willet P, Bar-Shalom Y. Tracking with converted position and Doppler measurements. In: Proceedings of SPIE Conference on Signal and Data Processing of Small Targets. 2011. pp. 4089-4094

[3] Bar-Shalom Y, Willett PK, Tian X. Tacking and Data Fusion: A Handbook of Algorithms. Storrs CT: YBS Publishing; 2011

[4] Duan Z, Han C, Li XR. Comments on unbiased converted measurements for tracking. IEEE Transactions on Aerospace and Electronic Systems. 2004;**40**(4):1374-1377. DOI: 10.1109/TAES.2004.1386889

[5] Fränken D. Consistent unbiased linear filtering with polar measurements. In: Proceedings of the 10th International Conference on Information Fusion. 2007. pp. 1-8

[6] Julier SJ, Uhlmann JK. A consistent, debiased method for converting between polar and Cartesian coordinate systems. In: Proceedings of the 1997 SPIE Conference on Acquisition, Tracking, and Pointing XI, 3086, SPIE. 1997. pp. 110-121

[7] Mei W, Bar-Shalom Y. Unbiased Kalman filter using converted measurements: Revisit. In: Proceedings of SPIE Conference on Signal and Data Processing of Small Targets 2009. pp. 7445:74450U-74450U-9

[8] Mo L, Song X, Zhou Y, Sun Z, Bar-Shalom Y. Unbiased converted measurements for tracking. IEEE Transactions on Aerospace and Electronic Systems. 1998;**34**(3): 1023-1027. DOI: 10.1109/7.705921

[9] Suchomski P. Explicit expressions for debiased statistics of 3D converted measurements. IEEE Transactions on Aerospace and Electronic Systems. 1999; **35**(1):368-370. DOI: 10.1109/7.745708

[10] Zhao ZL, Li XR, Jilkov VP, Zhu YM. Optimal linear unbiased filtering with polar measurements for target tracking. In: Proceedings of the 5th International Conference on Information Fusion, Annapolis, MD. 2002. pp. 1527-1534

[11] Bizup DF, Brown DE. The over-extended Kalman filter—don't use it. In: Proceedings of the 6th International Conference on Information Fusion, Cairns. Australia: Queensland; 2003. pp. 40-46

[12] Dai YP, Jin CZ, Hu JL, Hirasawa K, Liu Z. A target tracking algorithm with range rate under the color measurement environment. In: Proceedings of the 38th SICE Annual Conference. Japan: Morioka; 1999. pp. 1145-1148

[13] Duan Z, Han C, Li XR. Sequential nonlinear tracking filter with range-rate measurements in spherical coordinates. In: Proceedings of the 7th International Conference on Information Fusion. 2004. pp. 599-605

[14] Duan Z, Han C. Radar target tracking with range rate measurements in polar coordinates. Journal of System Simulation (Chinese). 2004;**16**(12): 2860-2863

[15] Duan Z, Li XR, Han C, Zhu H. Sequential unscented Kalman filter for radar target tracking with range rate measurements. In: Proceedings of the 8th International Conference on Information Fusion. 2005. pp. 130-137

[16] Kameda H, Tsujimichi S, Kosuge Y. Target tracking under dense environment using range rate measurements. In: Proceedings of the 37th SICE Annual Conference. Japan: Chiba; 1998. pp. 927-932

[17] Lei M, Han C. Sequential nonlinear tracking using UKF and raw range-rate measurements. IEEE Transactions on Aerospace and Electronic Systems. 2007;**43**(1):239-250. DOI: 10.1109/TAES.2007.357130

[18] Wang JG, Long T, He PK. Use of the radial velocity measurement in target tracking. IEEE Transactions on Aerospace and Electronic Systems. 2003;**39**(2):401-413. DOI: 10.1109/TAES.2003.1207253

[19] Park SE, Lee JG. Improved Kalman filter design for three-dimensional radar tracking. IEEE Transactions on Aerospace and Electronic Systems. 2001;**37**(2):727-739. DOI: 10.1109/7.937485

[20] Park ST, Lee JG. Design of a practical tracking algorithm with radar measurements. IEEE Transactions on Aerospace and Electronic Systems. 1998;**34**(4):1337-1344. DOI: 10.1109/7.722718

[21] Zollo S, Ristic B. On polar and versus Cartesian coordinates for target tracking. In: Proceedings of the 5th International Symposium on Signal Processing and its Applications. Australia: Brisbane; 1999. pp. 499-502

[22] Zhou G, Zhao N, Fu T, Quan T, Kirubarajan T. Enhanced sequential nonlinear tracking filter with denoised pseudo measurements. In: Proceedings of the 14th International Conference on Information Fusion, Chicago. USA: Illinois; 2011. pp. 1409-1415

[23] Zhou G, Yu C, Cui N, Quan T. A tracking filter in spherical coordinates enhanced by de-noising of converted Doppler measurements. Chinese Journal of Aeronautics. 2012;**25**(5):757-765

[24] Li XR, Jilkov VP. A survey of maneuvering target tracking-Part III: Measurement models. In: Proceedings of 2001 SPIE Conference on Signal and Data Processing of Small Targets, 4473, SPIE, San Diego, CA, USA. 2001. pp. 423-446

[25] Li XR, Jilkov VP. A survey of maneuvering target tracking-part I: Dynamics models. IEEE Transactions on Aerospace and Electronic Systems. 2003;**39**(4):1333-1364. DOI: 10.1109/TAES.2003.1261132

[26] Niu R, Willett P, Bar-Shalom Y. Tracking considerations in selection of radar waveform for range and range-rate measurements. IEEE Transactions on Aerospace and Electronic Systems. 2002;**38**(2):467-487. DOI: 10.1109/TAES.2002.1008980

[27] Zhou G, Pelletier M, Kirubarajan T, Quan T. Statically fused converted position and Doppler measurement Kalman filters. IEEE Transactions on Aerospace and Electronic Systems. 2014;**50**(1):300-318. DOI: 10.1109/TAES.2013.120256

[28] Zhou G, Wu L, Xie J, Deng W, Quan T. Constant turn model for statically fused converted measurement Kalman filters. Signal Processing. 2015;**108**(3):400-411. DOI: 10.1016/ j.sigpro.2014.09.022

[29] Zhou G, Guo Z, Chen X, Xu R, Kirubarajan T. Statically fused converted measurement Kalman filters for tracking with measurements of phased Array radars. IEEE Transactions on Aerospace and Electronic Systems. 2018;**54**(2):554-568. DOI: 10.1109/TAES.2017.2760798

Chapter 5

A Scalable, FPGA-Based Implementation of the Unscented Kalman Filter

Jeremy Soh and Xiaofeng Wu

Abstract

Autonomous aerospace systems may well soon become ubiquitous pending an increase in autonomous capability. Greater autonomous capability means there is a need for high-performance state estimation. However, the desire to reduce costs through simplified development processes and compact form factors can limit performance. A hardware-based approach, such as using a field-programmable gate array (FPGA), is common when high performance is required, but hardware approaches tend to have a more complicated development process when compared to traditional software approaches; greater development complexity, in turn, results in higher costs. Leveraging the advantages of both hardware-based and software-based approaches, a hardware/software (HW/SW) codesign of the unscented Kalman filter (UKF), based on an FPGA, is presented. The UKF is split into an application-specific part, implemented in software to simplify the development process, and a non-application-specific part, implemented in hardware as a parameterisable 'black box' module (i.e. IP core) to increase performance. Simulation results demonstrating a possible nanosatellite application of the design are presented; implementation (synthesis, timing, power) details are also presented.

Keywords: field-programmable gate array (FPGA), unscented Kalman filter (UKF), codesign, system on a chip (SoC), nonlinear state estimation

1. Introduction

Small (micro-, nano-, pico-) satellites and (micro-) unmanned aerial systems (UASs) are emerging technologies that have the potential to be of great academic and commercial use but only if a balance can be found between two diametrically opposed forces that act on their design: the desire, and need, for high performance and the desire to reduce costs. High performance, especially in state estimation, is necessary for these technologies to be advantageous over traditional aerospace systems in relevant applications.

The desire to reduce the costs of these technologies has led to their miniaturisation and heavy use of commercial off-the-shelf (COTS) components so that some level of economy of scale may be achieved. Though both component and development costs can be reduced in this way, this approach, in turn, leads to a reduction in the resources available (e.g. electrical power, computing power and physical space) aboard those systems, impacting performance.

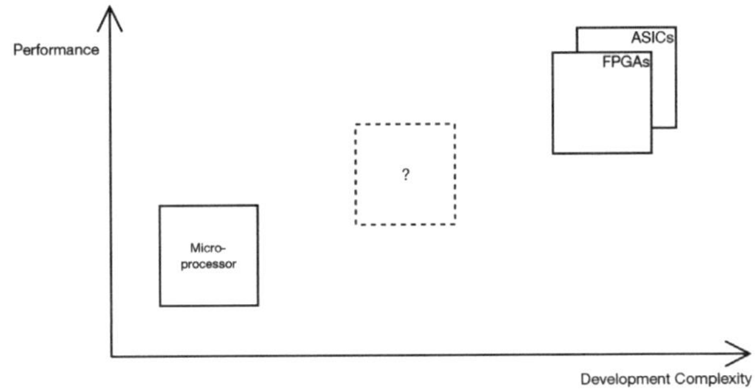

Figure 1.
The performance versus development complexity trade-off for different types of embedded systems.

Specialised hardware, e.g. application-specific integrated circuit (ASIC)- or field-programmable gate array (FPGA)-based systems, can achieve high performance, even for severely resource-constrained systems, but tends to increase the development complexity of these systems; in this way, using specialised hardware may reduce component costs and meet performance and miniaturisation requirements, while development costs are typically increased. This issue is illustrated in **Figure 1**, which depicts the balance between development complexity and performance for different embedded systems; greater complexity during the development process means that a greater investment in resources, personnel and time becomes necessary, which leads to higher development costs.

Software approaches, e.g. microprocessor-based systems, generally have lower performance than specialised hardware but have much simpler, and thus cheaper, development processes. It is, however, possible to draw upon aspects of both hardware and software approaches and combine them into a hardware/software codesign. This codesign could deliver the high performance of specialised hardware but, by using software techniques, e.g. modularity or abstraction, could also alleviate some of the high development costs associated with such hardware. If this codesign approach is applied to a prolific state estimation algorithm, then the performance and miniaturisation requirements could be met, while keeping development costs low.

In this chapter, a library containing a scalable, hardware/software (HW/SW) codesign of the unscented Kalman filter (UKF), based on an FPGA, is presented. The codesign is implemented as a fully parameterisable, self-contained 'black box' (which is often referred to as an IP core), which aims to minimise the necessary input from system designers when applying the codesign to a new application, such that overall development complexity is reduced.

This chapter is a distillation of work first presented in [1]. The rest of this chapter is organised as follows: Section 2 provides background on relevant concepts, Section 3 outlines the proposed design, Section 4 describes the simulation model to verify the design and simulation results, Section 5 presents implementation results and Section 6 concludes the chapter.

2. Background

2.1 Hardware/software codesign

Hardware/software codesign is a design practice that is often used with system-on-a-chip (SoC) architectures. The term system on a chip comes from the field of very large-scale integration (VLSI) where individual hardware units or 'black boxes' (IP cores) that perform some dedicated function are arranged and connected together on a single ASIC chip. Typical SoCs may include a microcontroller or microprocessor core, DSPs, memories such as RAMs or ROMs, peripherals such as timers/counters, communication interfaces such as USB/UART, analog interfaces such as ADCs/DACs or other analog, digital, mixed-signal or RF hardware. Previously, each of these components may have had its own ASIC and was connected together on a PCB, but, in accordance with Moore's law, resource densities of silicon chips have massively increased over time, so now these components are able to be integrated together on a single chip; an example SoC can be seen in **Figure 2a**.

(a) Example of a typical system on a chip.

(b) An example of a target architecture for early hardware/software codesign implementations.

SoC designs for FPGAs have become more popular recently as the increase in resource densities allowed more complex logic to be implemented. The push towards SoCs on FPGAs is driven by the desire for greater autonomy in a variety of systems; the most obvious example is field robotics, but autonomous systems such as 'smart' rooms and satellites also have a need for a small form factor and high-performance computing solutions that the FPGA is well placed to deliver.

As VLSI technology matured, designers began to see that the increase in development complexity for hardware or ASIC designs was impacting their ability to bring products to market quickly. The associated increase in the complexity of microprocessors led many designers to realise that these microprocessor units could be included into system designs and some of the functionality shifted to software to reduce their time to market. Microprocessors can be considered a SoC on their own, but they can also be included in much larger SoC designs, and this is where the idea of hardware/software codesign first began; reviews of the field by [2–4] give a comprehensive history of hardware/software codesign. A basic example of an architecture where hardware/software codesign may be appropriate is shown in **Figure 2b**.

2.2 Unscented Kalman filter

The extended Kalman filter (EKF) is, and has been, the most widespread method for nonlinear state estimation [5]. It has also become the de facto standard

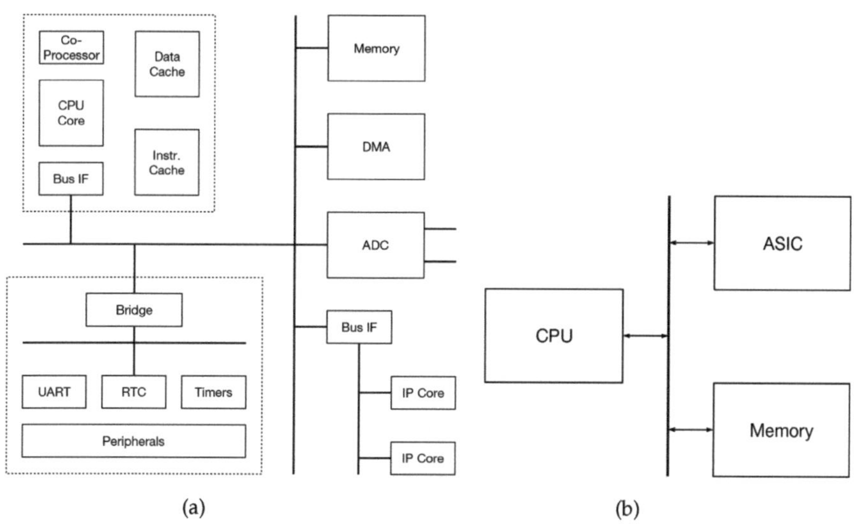

Figure 2.
Examples of system-on-a-chip architectures.

by which other methods are compared when analysing their performance. Various surveys of the field have noted that the EKF is 'unquestionably dominant' [6], 'the workhorse' of state estimation [7, 8] and the 'most common' nonlinear filter [9]. Despite some shortcomings, the relative ease of implementation and still-remarkable accuracy have propelled the EKF's popularity.

However, more recently the unscented Kalman filter (UKF) [10] has been shown to perform much better than the EKF when the system models are 'highly' nonlinear [6–9, 11]. While the EKF attempts to deal with non-linearities in the system model by using the Jacobian to linearise the system model, the UKF instead models the current state as a probability distribution with some mean and covariance. Following this, a deterministic sampling technique known as the unscented transform (UT) is applied. A set of points, called 'sigma' points, are drawn from the probability distribution, and each of them propagated through the nonlinear system models. The new mean and covariance of the transformed sigma points are then recovered to inform the new state estimate. The crucial aspect of the UT is that the sigma points are drawn deterministically, unlike random sampling methods like Monte Carlo algorithms, drastically reducing the number of points necessary to recover the 'transformed' mean and covariance.

Consider the general nonlinear system described for discrete time, k:

$$\mathbf{x}_k = f(\mathbf{x}_{k-1}, \mathbf{u}_{k-1}, \mathbf{w}_{k-1}) \tag{1}$$

$$\mathbf{z}_k = h(\mathbf{x}_k, \mathbf{v}_k) \tag{2}$$

where f and h are the system's process and observation models, respectively; $\mathbf{x}$ and $\mathbf{z}$ are the state and observation vectors, respectively; $\mathbf{u}$ is the control input and $\mathbf{w}$ and $\mathbf{v}$ are, respectively, the process/control and measurement/observation noise, which are assumed to be zero-mean Gaussian white noise terms with covariances $\mathbf{Q}$ and $\mathbf{R}$. The formalisation of the UKF for this system is as follows. Define an augmented state vector, $\mathbf{x}^a$, with length M that concatenates the process/control noise and measurement noise terms with the state variables as

$$\mathbf{x}_k^a = \begin{bmatrix} \mathbf{x}_k \\ \mathbf{w}_k \\ \mathbf{v}_k \end{bmatrix} \tag{3}$$

The augmented state vector has an associated augmented state covariance, $\mathbf{P}_k^a$, which combines the (regular) state covariance, $\mathbf{P}_k$, with the noise covariances $\mathbf{Q}_k$ and $\mathbf{R}_k$. The augmented state vector and covariance are initialised with

$$\begin{gathered} \hat{\mathbf{x}}_0^a = E\left[\mathbf{x}_0^a\right] = \begin{bmatrix} \hat{\mathbf{x}}_0 \\ \mathbf{0} \\ \mathbf{0} \end{bmatrix} \\ \mathbf{P}_0^a = E\left[\left(\mathbf{x}_0^a - \hat{\mathbf{x}}_0^a\right)\left(\mathbf{x}_0^a - \hat{\mathbf{x}}_0^a\right)^T\right] = \begin{bmatrix} \mathbf{P}_0 & 0 & 0 \\ 0 & \mathbf{Q}_0 & 0 \\ 0 & 0 & \mathbf{R}_0 \end{bmatrix} \end{gathered} \tag{4}$$

where $\hat{\mathbf{x}}_0$ is the expected value of the initial (regular) state. There exist various other sigma point selection strategies, and, in order to minimise computational effort, a selection strategy involving a minimal set of samples is highly desired. The spherical simplex set of points [10, 12] can be shown to offer similar performance to the original UKF with the smallest number of sigma points required ($M+2$). The sigma point weights, and a coefficient matrix is generated by choosing $0 \le W_0 \le 1$ and then calculating W_1:

$$W_1 = W_i = \frac{(1-W_0)}{(M+1)} \qquad i = 1, \dots, M+1 \tag{5}$$

The choice of W_0 determines the spread of sigma points about the mean. Choosing $W_0 \approx 1$ reduces the spread, implying a greater confidence in the previous estimate, while the opposite is true when choosing $W_0 \approx 0$. The vector sequence is initialised as

$$\boldsymbol{\sigma}_0^1 = [0], \ \ \boldsymbol{\sigma}_1^1 = -\left[\frac{1}{\sqrt{2W_1}}\right], \ \ \boldsymbol{\sigma}_2^1 = \left[\frac{1}{\sqrt{2W_1}}\right] \tag{6}$$

Then, the vector sequence is expanded for $j = 2, \dots, M$ via

$$\boldsymbol{\sigma}_i^j = \begin{cases} \begin{bmatrix} \boldsymbol{\sigma}_0^{j-1} \\ 0 \end{bmatrix} & i = 0 \\ \begin{bmatrix} \boldsymbol{\sigma}_i^{j-1} \\ -\dfrac{1}{\sqrt{j(j+1)W_1}} \end{bmatrix} & i = 1, \dots, j \\ \begin{bmatrix} \mathbf{0}_{j-1} \\ \dfrac{j}{\sqrt{j(j+1)W_1}} \end{bmatrix} & i = j+1 \end{cases} \tag{7}$$

The actual sigma points are drawn, via a column-wise accumulation, from

$$\chi_{i,k} = \hat{\mathbf{x}}_k^a + \left(\sqrt{\mathbf{P}_k^a}\boldsymbol{\sigma}\right)_i \tag{8}$$

where i refers to the ith column of the matrix product and $\sqrt{\mathbf{P}_k^a}$ refers to the matrix 'square root'. The matrix square root of a target matrix $\mathbf{A}$ is a matrix $\mathbf{B}$ that satisfies $\mathbf{A} = \mathbf{BB}$; it is often calculated via the Cholesky decomposition [13].

The `predict` step begins with the sigma points being propagated through the system model:

$$\chi_{i,k|k-1}^x = f\left(\chi_{i,k-1|k-1}^x, \mathbf{u}_{k-1|k-1}, \chi_{i,k-1|k-1}^w\right) \tag{9}$$

The state and covariance are then predicted as

$$\hat{\mathbf{x}}_k^- = \sum_{i=0}^{N-1} W_i^{(m)} \chi_{i,k|k-1}^x \tag{10}$$

$$\mathbf{P}_k^- = \sum_{i=0}^{N-1} W_i^{(c)} \left[\chi_{i,k|k-1}^x - \hat{\mathbf{x}}_k^-\right]\left[\chi_{i,k|k-1}^x - \hat{\mathbf{x}}_k^-\right]^T \tag{11}$$

For the `update` step, the sigma points that were updated in the `predict` step are propagated through the observation model:

$$\mathcal{Z}_{i,k|k-1} = h\left(\chi_{i,k|k-1}^x, \chi_{i,k-1|k-1}^v\right) \tag{12}$$

The mean and covariance of the observation-transformed sigma points are calculated:

$$\hat{\mathbf{z}}_{k|k-1} = \sum_{i=0}^{N-1} W_i^{(m)} \mathcal{Z}_{i,k|k-1} \tag{13}$$

$$\mathbf{S}_{k|k-1} = \sum_{i=0}^{N-1} W_i^{(c)} \left[\chi_{i,\,k|k-1} - \hat{\mathbf{z}}_{k|k-1}\right]\left[\mathcal{Z}_{i,k|k-1} - \hat{\mathbf{z}}_{k|k-1}\right]^T \tag{14}$$

followed by the cross-covariance

$$\mathbf{P}_{xz,\,k|k-1} = \sum_{i=0}^{N-1} W_i^{(c)} \left[\chi_{i,\,k|k-1}^{x} - \hat{\mathbf{x}}_{k|k-1}^{-}\right]\left[\mathcal{Z}_{i,k|k-1} - \hat{\mathbf{z}}_{k|k-1}\right]^T \tag{15}$$

and the Kalman gain

$$\mathbf{K} = \mathbf{P}_{xz,\,k|k-1}\mathbf{S}_{k|k-1}^{-1} \tag{16}$$

Finally, the current system state is estimated by

$$\hat{\mathbf{x}}_k = \hat{\mathbf{x}}_{k|k-1}^{-} + \mathbf{K}\left(\tilde{\mathbf{z}}_k - \hat{\mathbf{z}}_{k|k-1}\right) \tag{17}$$

where $\tilde{\mathbf{z}}$ is the current set of observations and the current covariance is updated with

$$\mathbf{P}_k = \mathbf{P}_{k|k-1}^{-} - \mathbf{K}\mathbf{S}_{k|k-1}\mathbf{K}^T \tag{18}$$

$$= \mathbf{P}_{k|k-1}^{-} - \mathbf{P}_{xz,\,k|k-1}\mathbf{K}^T \tag{19}$$

where the expression for the Kalman gain, Eq. (16), is substituted.

3. Hardware/software codesign of the unscented Kalman filter

The first exercise in the hardware/software codesign is to divide the UKF algorithm into two parts. For maximum performance, it is desirable for as much of the algorithm as possible to be implemented in hardware. However, to maintain portability, any part of the algorithm that is application-specific would be better implemented in software. This is so that the application-specific parts can make use of the faster and simpler development processes that using software entails. Reviewing the UKF algorithm, only the two system models, the `predict` and `update` models, are application-specific.

Apart from the two system models, the rest of the UKF can be viewed as, essentially, a series of matrix manipulations. The only changes to the rest of the UKF when either of the system models changes are the size of the vectors and matrices used in the UKF calculations. The sizes of these vectors and matrices are fixed for a particular formulation of the UKF, and so they can be treated as parameters that are set at synthesis. Fixing the parameters at synthesis means that only the bare minimum of hardware resources is needed, but the hardware can still be easily used for different applications with different vector/matrix sizes; rather than needing to redesign any functionality, the hardware can simply be synthesised with different parameters. Thus, the rest of the UKF can be designed and then used as a parameterisable, modular 'black box' (IP core), and implementing it for any given application only requires the appropriate selection of parameters.

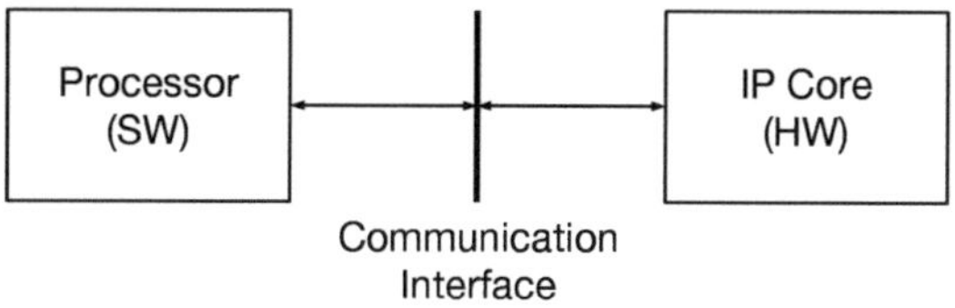

Figure 3.
The hardware/software partition on the FPGA.

When it comes to designing hardware, there are three main considerations: the performance of the hardware (which may include data throughput, maximum clock frequency, etc.), the logic area (on-chip resources) used and the power consumption of the hardware. During development these considerations are usually at odds with each other—specifically performance is usually opposed by logic area and power consumption. In order to increase the performance of the design, additional resources often have to be used which, in turn, may increase the power consumption; these increases in resource/power cost may make the implementation infeasible for a given application. Due to these considerations, it is beneficial to give system designers the ability to scale resource use to the requirements of their particular application.

The actual physical implementation of the hardware/software UKF on an FPGA can be seen in **Figure 3**. The hardware part is implemented as a stand-alone IP core, and the software part is implemented on a general-purpose microprocessor. The processor acts as the main controller which, in addition to implementing the system model software, controls the hardware IP core. The precise method of controlling the IP core is dependent on the design variation and is elaborated on in the following sections.

The processor communicates with the IP core over some communication interface. Any intra-chip communication method would be sufficient and would be driven mostly by the requirements of the application; viable interfaces include point-to-point, bus or NoC interfaces. The IP core contains memory buffers at the interface in order to receive data from the processor as well as to temporarily store data that needs to be read by the processor. The communication interface is the same between all three variants, but the specifics of the memory buffers are not.

Here, the communication interface between the two parts is an AXI4 bus. All variants are implemented using single-precision arithmetic (IEEE-754); this gives a decent balance of dynamic range and resource usage which should be sufficient for the majority of applications. All hardware in the codesign is developed using the Verilog HDL, and all software in the codesign is developed using C. Although C is used here, in general, any type of software may be used as long as it contains the ability to interact with the communication interface connecting the hardware and software parts.

3.1 Overall design

The codesign utilises the main benefit of hardware implementations: wide parallelism. An increase in performance is gained by encapsulating certain parts of the major datapaths into a sub-module called a processing element (PE) and then using multiple instances of these PEs in parallel, allowing multiple elements of an algorithm to be calculated at once. The increase in resources used is not only for the extra processing elements but also in the additional overhead needed to deal with the parallel memory structure that is also necessary to feed to the parallel processing elements. The number of PEs used in the design is parameterisable, allowing for some trade-offs by the system designer between resources used and performance.

The codesign logically separates the UKF algorithm into three parts, while on the hardware side, the IP core consists of the UKF hardware and a memory buffer which is attached to a communication (AXI4) bus; the top-level block diagram of the codesign can be seen in **Figure 4**. The memory buffer has a memory map that ensures that data are coherent between the processor and the IP core and also incorporate a control register which allows the IP core to be controlled. The control register allows the processor to reset or enable the IP core as a whole as well as start one of the core's functional steps via a state machine; the control register also records the current state of the IP core. Data required by the IP core (e.g. transformed sigma points) must be placed in the memory buffer at the appropriate address by the processor before signalling the IP core to begin its calculations. The control register may be polled by the processor to control the IP core; alternatively, the core may also be configured with an optional interrupt line that may be attached to the processor's interrupt controller or external interrupt lines.

3.2 Sigma point generation

The sig_gen step uses the current augmented state vector and covariance to calculate the new sigma points via (Eq. (8)). To calculate the new set of sigma points, first the matrix 'square root' of the current augmented covariance must be calculated which is implemented by the trisolve module. The 'square root' of the augmented covariance is then multiplied by the sigma coefficients weighting matrix and the current augmented state vector added column-wise; this is implemented by the matrix multiply-add module described in Section 3.2.2. After the sigma points are calculated, they are written to the memory buffer; a control bit is set to signify completion to the processor; and if the interrupt line is included, an interrupt generated. A block diagram of this step can be seen in **Figure 5** showing the data flow between modules.

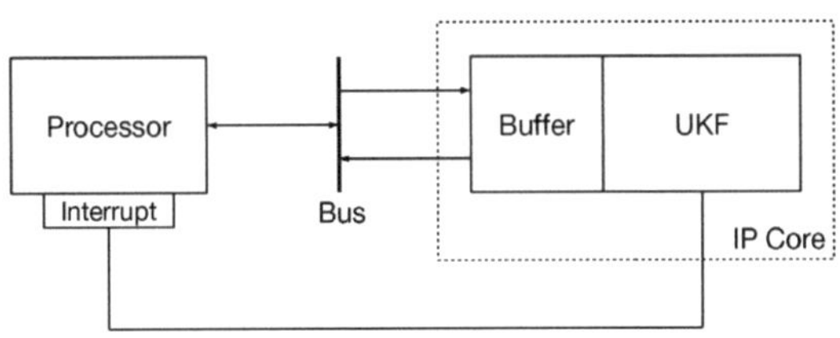

Figure 4.
Top-level block diagram.

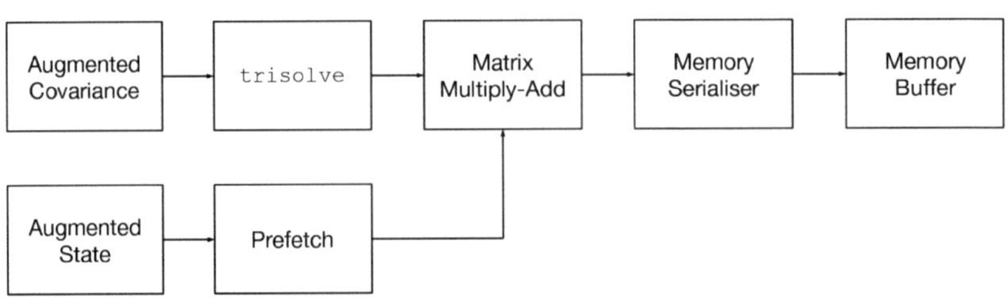

Figure 5.
Block diagram of the sig_gen *step.*

The memory prefetch and memory serialiser modules add a small amount of overhead to the `sig_gen` step but are necessary due to the matrix multiply-add featuring a parallelised datapath but the memory buffer requiring serial access.

3.2.1 Triangular linear equation solver

In addition to the matrix 'square root', the Cholesky decomposition is also used in the Kalman gain calculation which involves a matrix inversion (see Eq. (16)). Directly computing a matrix inversion is extremely computationally demanding; so rather than directly inverting the matrix, an algorithm called the matrix 'right divide' is used here. For positive definite matrices, this algorithm involves using the Cholesky decomposition to decompose the target matrix into a triangular form followed by forward elimination and then back substitution to solve the system; this sequence may be treated as solving a series of triangular linear equations meaning the same hardware can be reused for each operation [14]. The Cholesky decomposition of a target matrix **A**, which is positive definite, is given by

$$\mathbf{A} = \mathbf{L}_1\mathbf{L}_1^T \tag{20}$$

where $\mathbf{L}_1$ is lower triangular. Reducing the calculation to a series of triangular linear equations involves using an alternative version:

$$\mathbf{A} = \mathbf{L}_2\mathbf{D}\mathbf{L}_2^T \tag{21}$$

where $\mathbf{L}_2$ is lower triangular and its diagonal terms are unit elements, **D** is diagonal and the two versions are related by

$$\mathbf{L}_1 = \mathbf{L}_2\sqrt{\mathbf{D}} \tag{22}$$

The recombination process is necessary because of the subsequent matrix multiply-add between the augmented covariance square root and the sigma weighting coefficient matrix (see Eq. (8)). The element-wise calculation for $\mathbf{L}_2$ and **D** is given by

$$F_{ij} = \left(A_{ij} - \sum_{k=1}^{j-1} L_{ik}F_{jk}\right) \quad \text{for } i>j \tag{23}$$

$$D_j = A_{jj} - \sum_{k=1}^{j-1} \frac{F_{jk}^2}{D_k} \tag{24}$$

where $F_{ij} = L_{ij}D_j$ and $F_{jk} = L_{jk}D_k$ are substituted to simplify the calculation further. **Figure 6** depicts the full `trisolve` datapath, including the division and the recombination process to recover $\mathbf{L}_1$. The input b is either A_{ij} in the Cholesky decomposition or an element from the divisor matrix in the matrix 'right divide'.

The fused multiply-add module and feedback FIFO have been encapsulated to form an elementary block of hardware called a processing element (PE) which can be instantiated multiple times in parallel. The PE output to a demultiplexer, which ensures values, is passed to the subsequent calculations in the correct order. The latter calculations, after the demultiplexer, are not parallelised because these calculations require much fewer operations, and so parallelisation is not necessary.

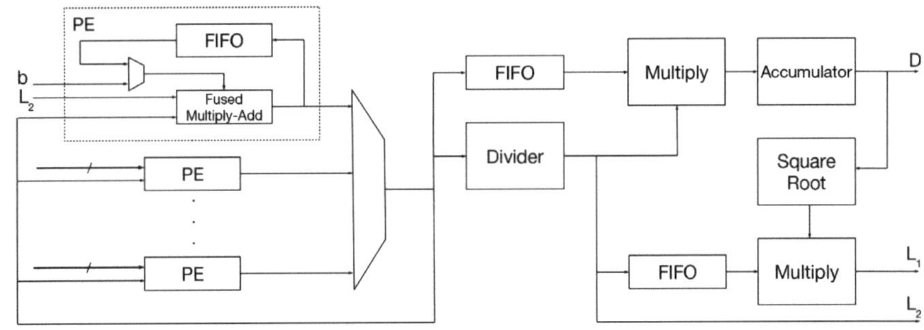

Figure 6.
Triangular linear equation solver.

3.2.2 Matrix multiply-add

The matrix multiply-add datapath is a standard 'naive' element-wise multiplication and accumulation. However, the hardware to calculate one element is enclosed as one processing element, and additional PEs are added to handle calculations in parallel; the matrix multiply-add datapath can be seen in **Figure 7**. Each PE is responsible for calculating at least one row of the result matrix. The elements of the matrix to be added can simply be injected into the accumulation directly, instead of performing an additional matrix addition after a matrix multiplication.

3.3 Predict step

The `predict` step uses the transformed sigma points to calculate the a priori state estimate; the architecture for the `predict` step can be seen in **Figure 8** showing how data flows between each module.

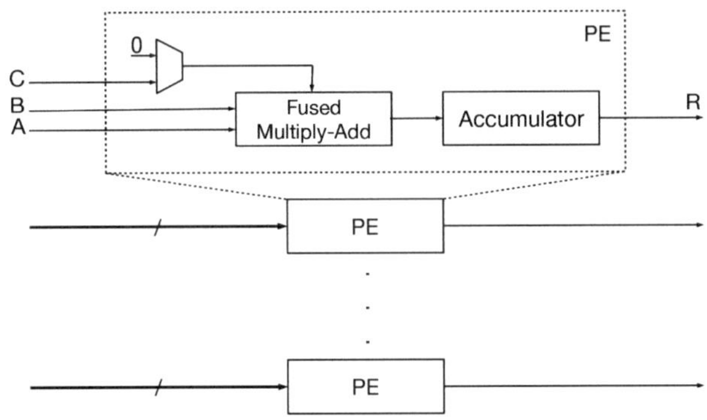

Figure 7.
Matrix multiply-add operation.

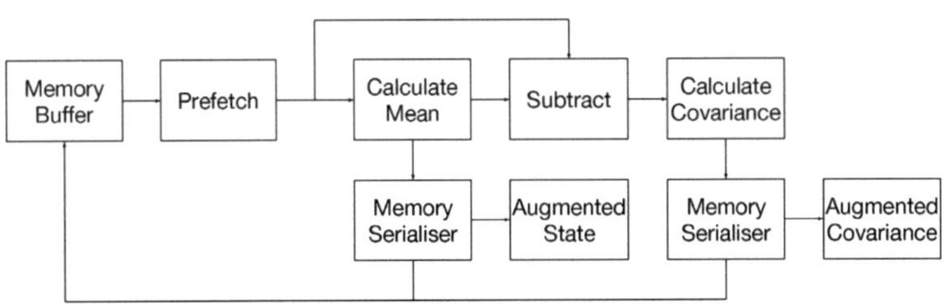

Figure 8.
Block diagram of the predict step.

The processor may initiate a `predict` step once it has placed valid transformed sigma points into the memory buffer. The prefetch module fetches the transformed sigma points from the memory buffer and places them into a parallel memory structure. The mean of the transformed sigma points is calculated which is also the a priori state estimate (10). The transformed sigma points and the mean are then used to calculate the 'sigma point residuals' via a `subtract` operation. From the 'sigma point residuals', the covariance of the set of transformed sigma points is calculated which is also the a priori covariance (11). Calculation of the mean and covariance is implemented by the calculate mean/covariance module described in Section 3.3.1; this section also describes the details of the 'sigma point residuals'. Once the calculations are complete, the IP core writes the a priori state and covariance to the memory buffer so that both the processor and IP core have the current state estimate. Once the `predict` step is completed, a control bit is set to notify the processor, and, if included, an interrupt generated.

3.3.1 Calculation of mean/covariance

Calculating the mean and covariance of the transformed sigma points is both very similar, meaning both can be calculated by the same datapath. Consider the calculation for the mean of the `predict` step transformed sigma points:

$$\hat{\mathbf{x}}_k^- = \sum_{i=1}^{N} W_i \chi_i^x \tag{25}$$

This is a simple column-wise multiply-accumulation. Consider the calculation of the covariance:

$$\mathbf{P}_k^- = \sum_{i=1}^{N} W_i \left[\chi_i^x - \hat{\mathbf{x}}^-\right]\left[\chi_i^x - \hat{\mathbf{x}}^-\right]^T \tag{26}$$

The subtraction looks like it will cause inefficiencies in the datapath, similar to the division operation in the original Cholesky decomposition. However, let $\tilde{\chi}_i = \chi_i^x - \hat{\mathbf{x}}^-$ be the ith column of $\tilde{\chi}$, and then the covariance calculation reduces to

$$\mathbf{P}_k^- = \sum_{i=1}^{N} W_i \tilde{\chi}_i \tilde{\chi}_i^T \tag{27}$$

This 'sigma point residual' matrix $\tilde{\chi}$ is of size $M_{state} \times N$ where M_{state} is the number of state variables and $N = M + 2$ is the number of sigma points. The element-wise calculation is then

$$P_{ij}^- = \sum_{k=1}^{N} W_1 \tilde{\chi}_{ik} \tilde{\chi}_{jk} \tag{28}$$

This expression involves two multiplications followed by an accumulation; if these 'sigma point residuals' are calculated first with a `subtract` operation, then both the mean and covariance calculations simply involve a series of multiplications and accumulation. Similar to the matrix multiply-add operation, the basic calculations are encapsulated into one processing element, and then additional PEs are added to the datapath in order to calculate additional rows in parallel; the datapath can be seen in **Figure 9**.

The input to the datapath is either the transformed sigma points to calculate the mean or the residuals to calculate the covariance. The FIFO is used to skip the first

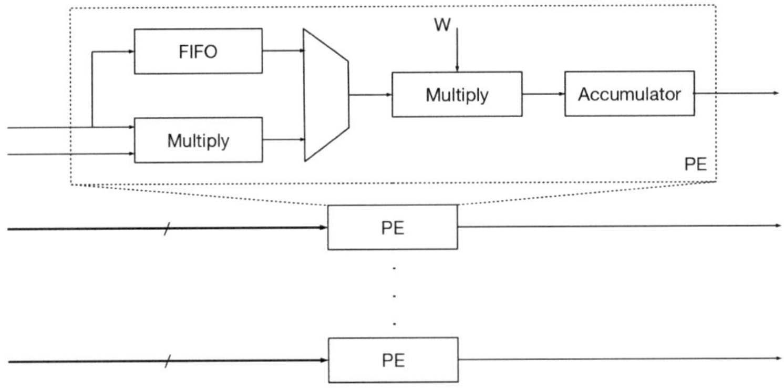

Figure 9.
Calculate mean/covariance operation. W refers the sigma point weights W_0, W_1.

multiplication when calculating the mean; the multiplexer selects which value is calculated.

3.4 Update step

The `update` step corrects the a priori state estimate with a set of observations to generate the new state estimate. Many of the calculations in the `update` step are very similar to the `predict` step; the architecture for the `update` step can be seen in **Figure 10** showing the data flow between modules.

As with the `predict` step, the processor must first place the valid transformed sigma points into the memory buffer before signalling the IP core to begin. First, the prefetch module converts the transformed sigma points into a parallel memory structure. The mean and 'sigma point residuals' are calculated and then used to calculate the observation covariance. The `update` 'sigma point residuals' are also combined with the `predict` 'sigma point residuals', which were calculated during the `predict` step, to calculate the cross-covariance between the two system models. The observation residual, $\tilde{\mathbf{z}} - \hat{\mathbf{z}}$ (17), is calculated with the current set of observations in the memory buffer. The observation and cross-covariance are used to calculate the Kalman gain before the matrix multiply-add modules use the Kalman gain and the a priori state estimate and covariance to calculate the new state estimate and covariance. The new estimates overwrite the a priori estimates in the internal memory and are also written into the memory buffer such that both the core and the processor have the most recent estimate. The core notifies the processor upon completion, setting a control bit and/or generating an interrupt.

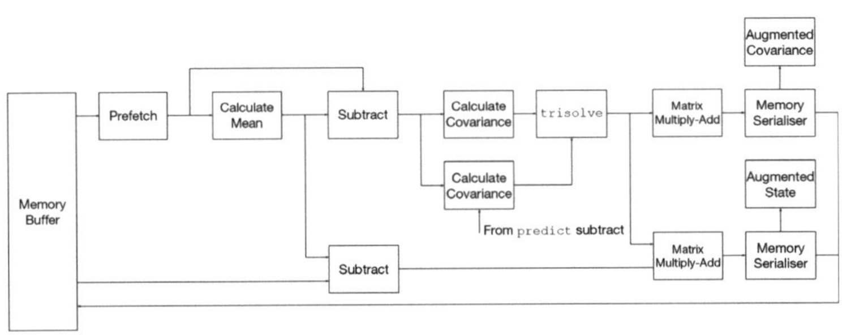

Figure 10.
Block diagram of the update step.

4. Testing and validation of the hardware/software codesign

To validate the implementation of the hardware/software UKF and demonstrate its effectiveness, an example application is presented. This demonstration emulates the attitude determination subsystem of a single, uncontrolled nanosatellite. It is envisioned that a system designer looking to use the HW/SW UKF in a new application simply formulates the UKF appropriately for that application, i.e. formulates the system models (1), (2) and sets the algorithm parameters. Then, once the UKF algorithm has been defined, the HW/SW codesign detailed in Section 3 can then be used to actually implement the UKF and accelerate its performance. The example application attempts to employ this process.

The UKF was implemented using a number of methods for validation and comparison purposes. Once formulated, the UKF was first implemented in MATLAB (SW) to validate the design of the UKF algorithm. Next, the UKF was implemented again using the HW/SW codesign on an FPGA development board in order to validate the codesign. Finally, the UKF was implemented a third time in C (SW), but on the same FPGA development board, to provide a performance benchmark the HW/SW codesign could be compared to.

The FPGA development board used was the Zedboard, featuring a Xilinx Zynq-7000 series XC7Z020, seen in **Figure 11**. The relevant features of the board are:

- Dual ARM Cortex-A9 processor system (PS) @ 667 MHz
- The equivalent of an Artix-7 device in programmable logic (PL)
- AXI4 PS-PL interface

The HW/SW codesign was implemented for the 1 PE and 2 PE cases. The hardware part of the codesign, the IP core, was developed in Verilog and synthesised and implemented using Vivado 2014.1; basic arithmetic was implemented using floating point IP cores from Xilinx's IP catalogue. All designs used a single-precision (IEEE 754–2008) number representation. The target synthesisable frequency for the IP core was 100 MHz, and the 2 PE case instantiated two processing elements for the whole design (i.e. each individual module had two processing elements). The software part of the codesign was implemented in C as bare-metal application on the processor system. The general-purpose AXI4

Figure 11.
Zedboard development board used for two of the UKF implementations.

interface between the PS and the PL was used by the two parts to communicate with each other (@ 100 MHz as well). The C (SW) implementation of the UKF was a bare-metal application that used the GNU Scientific Library (GSL) for its vector and matrix manipulations. All software was compiled using the -O2 optimisation flag.

To test the different UKF implementations, a simulator was constructed in MATLAB to model the nanosatellite's motion; the details are given in Section 4.5. Simulated sensor measurements were generated from the nanosatellites' motion and passed to each of the three UKF implementations, which act as the attitude determination subsystem. For the MATLAB implementation, the simulated measurements could be passed directly. For the HW/SW codesign and the C (SW) implementations, the simulated measurements were first exported to a C header which was included during compilation.

4.1 System model

The nanosatellite is modelled as a 1 U CubeSat. The attitude of the nanosatellite is represented by the unit quaternion $q = \left[\mathbf{q}, q_0\right]^T$ where $\mathbf{q} = \left[q_1, q_2, q_3\right]^T$ and which satisfies $q_1^2 + q_2^2 + q_3^2 + q_0^2 = 1$.

The kinematic equations for the satellite in terms of quaternions are given by

$$\dot{\mathbf{q}} = \frac{1}{2}\left(q_0 I_{3\times3} + \mathbf{q}^\times\right)\boldsymbol{\omega} \tag{29}$$

$$\dot{q}_0 = -\frac{1}{2}\mathbf{q}^T\boldsymbol{\omega} \tag{30}$$

where $\boldsymbol{\omega}$ is the angular rate and $\mathbf{q}^\times$ is the skew-symmetric matrix of $\mathbf{q}$ given by

$$\mathbf{q}^\times = \begin{bmatrix} 0 & -q_3 & q_2 \\ q_3 & 0 & -q_1 \\ -q_2 & q_1 & 0 \end{bmatrix} \tag{31}$$

4.2 Sensor model

We consider a basic sensor set common on nanosatellites—a three-axis MEMS IMU including an accelerometer, gyroscope and magnetometer. We use the standard gyroscopic model for the gyroscope:

$$\mathbf{z}_g = \boldsymbol{\omega}_T + \boldsymbol{\beta} + \boldsymbol{\eta}_g \tag{32}$$

$$\dot{\boldsymbol{\beta}} = \boldsymbol{\eta}_d \tag{33}$$

where $\boldsymbol{\omega}_T$ is the true angular velocity, $\boldsymbol{\beta}$ is the gyroscopic bias, $\dot{\boldsymbol{\beta}}$ is the gyroscopic bias drift and $\boldsymbol{\eta}_g$, $\boldsymbol{\eta}_d$ are noise terms that are assumed to be zero-mean Gaussians. Similarly, we model the accelerometer and magnetometer as

$$\mathbf{z}_a = \mathbf{a}_T + \boldsymbol{\eta}_a \tag{34}$$

$$\mathbf{z}_m = \mathbf{m}_T + \boldsymbol{\eta}_m \tag{35}$$

where $\mathbf{a}_T$ is the true local acceleration vector, $\mathbf{m}_T$ is the true local magnetic vector and $\boldsymbol{\eta}_a$, $\boldsymbol{\eta}_m$ are, again, zero-mean Gaussian measurement noise terms.

4.3 Predict model

We use a dead-reckoning model and the gyroscopic data to predict the motion of the nanosatellite. However, it is necessary to account for the gyroscopic bias drift, so we estimate the current gyroscopic bias as well. Let the state vector be

$$\mathbf{x} = \left[\mathbf{q}, q_0, \boldsymbol{\beta}\right]^T \tag{36}$$

The predict model, f, is then

$$f\left(\mathcal{X}^x_{k-1|k-1}, \mathcal{X}^w_{k-1|k-1}\right) = \mathcal{X}^x_{k-1|k-1} + f'\left(\mathcal{X}^x_{k-1|k-1}, \mathcal{X}^w_{k-1|k-1}\right) \cdot dt \tag{37}$$

$$f'\left(\mathcal{X}^x_{k-1|k-1}, \mathcal{X}^w_{k-1|k-1}\right) = \begin{bmatrix} \frac{1}{2}\left(q_0 I_{3\times3} + \mathbf{q}^\times\right)\mathbf{z}_g \\ -\frac{1}{2}\mathbf{q}^T\mathbf{z}_g \\ \mathbf{0}_{3\times1} \end{bmatrix} + \mathbf{w}_k \tag{38}$$

where dt is the time step between samples, $\mathbf{w}_k = \left[\boldsymbol{\eta}_q, \dot{\boldsymbol{\beta}}\right]^T$ is the process noise and $\boldsymbol{\eta}_q$ is assumed to be a zero-mean Gaussian.

4.4 Update model

The accelerometer and magnetometer data are used to correct for the gyroscopic bias, so the observation model, h, is

$$h\left(\mathcal{X}^x_{k-1|k-1}, \mathcal{X}^v_{k-1|k-1}\right) = \begin{bmatrix} A_q(\mathbf{q})g\mathbf{b}_a \\ A_q(\mathbf{q})\mathbf{b}_m \end{bmatrix} + \mathbf{v}_k \tag{39}$$

where $\mathbf{b}_a$ and $\mathbf{b}_m$ are the respective body frame vectors, g is the magnitude of the gravity vector (assumed 8.94 m.s^{-2} at an altitude of 300 km), $\mathbf{v}_k = [\boldsymbol{\eta}_a, \boldsymbol{\eta}_m]$ is the measurement noise and $A_q(\mathbf{q})$ is the rotation matrix between the body frame and the local frame given by

$$A_q(\mathbf{q}) = \begin{bmatrix} q_0^2 + q_1^2 - q_2^2 - q_3^2 & 2(q_1q_2 - q_0q_3) & 2(q_0q_2 + q_1q_3) \\ 2(q_1q_2 + q_0q_3) & q_0^2 - q_1^2 + q_2^2 - q_3^2 & 2(q_2q_3 - q_0q_1) \\ 2(q_1q_3 - q_0q_2) & 2(q_0q_1 + q_2q_3) & q_0^2 - q_1^2 - q_2^2 + q_3^2 \end{bmatrix} \tag{40}$$

4.5 Simulation model

Collecting all the relevant terms, the initial augmented state vector is given by

$$\mathbf{x}^a_0 = \left[\mathbf{q}, q_0, \boldsymbol{\beta}, \mathbf{0}_{4\times1}, \mathbf{0}_{3\times1}, \mathbf{0}_{3\times1}, \mathbf{0}_{3\times1}\right]^T, \tag{41}$$

and the initial augmented covariance is a diagonal matrix with diagonal terms:

$$\mathrm{diag}\left(\mathbf{P}^a_0\right) = \left[\mathbf{1}_{6\times1}, \boldsymbol{\eta}_q, \dot{\boldsymbol{\beta}}, \boldsymbol{\eta}_a, \boldsymbol{\eta}_m\right] \tag{42}$$

The state vector length is 7, the number of observation variables is 6 and the augmented state vector length is 20. The quaternion noise term was modelled with covariance $\boldsymbol{\eta}_q = 10^{-6}$. The simulated sensor set was homogeneous, so the modelled errors are the same for each nanosatellite. The gyroscopic bias drift was modelled with covariance $\boldsymbol{\eta}_d = 10^{-2^\circ}/s^2$. The measurement noise terms were modelled with covariances: $\boldsymbol{\eta}_g = 10^{-1^\circ}/s$, $\boldsymbol{\eta}_a = 10^{-2}g$, $\boldsymbol{\eta}_m = 10^{-2}\,gauss$. The satellite was modelled as undergoing slow tumbling. The motion was modelled using the Euler angles in a local ground frame, which is relevant in most remote sensing applications; here, we use roll-pitch-yaw to refer to rotations about the x-y-z axis, respectively.

To generate the sensor measurements, the simulated motions were converted into the body frame via rotation matrix with 1–2-3 referring to roll-pitch-yaw, respectively:

$$A_{euler} = \begin{bmatrix} c_1c_2 & c_1s_2s_3 - s_1c_3 & s_1s_3 + c_1s_2c_3 \\ s_1c_2 & s_1s_2s_3 + c_1c_3 & s_1s_2s_3 - c_1s_3 \\ -s_2 & c_2s_3 & c_2c_3 \end{bmatrix} \tag{43}$$

It is assumed that the magnetometer is aligned with the x-axis ($\mathbf{b}_m = [1, 0, 0]$) and the accelerometer is aligned with the z-axis ($\mathbf{b}_a = [0, 0, 1]$). Next, using the sensor models described earlier, noise terms were added to the sensor 'truth' data which was then sampled at 1 Hz to simulate measurements from an actual set of sensors.

4.6 Results

The UKF was simulated in MATLAB environment as well as on the Zedboard development board. For the Zedboard implementations, the simulated sensor data set was loaded into the onboard memory (RAM) and the UKF simulated as if it were receiving data from the actual sensors. The data set used in all three implementations was the same. State estimates from the UKF were stored on the Zedboard for the duration of the simulation and then read back into MATLAB afterwards for analysis.

All three implementations produced (within working precision) the simulation results in **Figure 12a** and **b**; these figures show the absolute attitude error (i.e. the difference between the UKF estimated attitude and the simulated 'truth') of the nanosatellite. In **Figure 12a**, the top graph shows the first tenth of a second of the simulation, highlighting early convergence of the filter to the truth from an

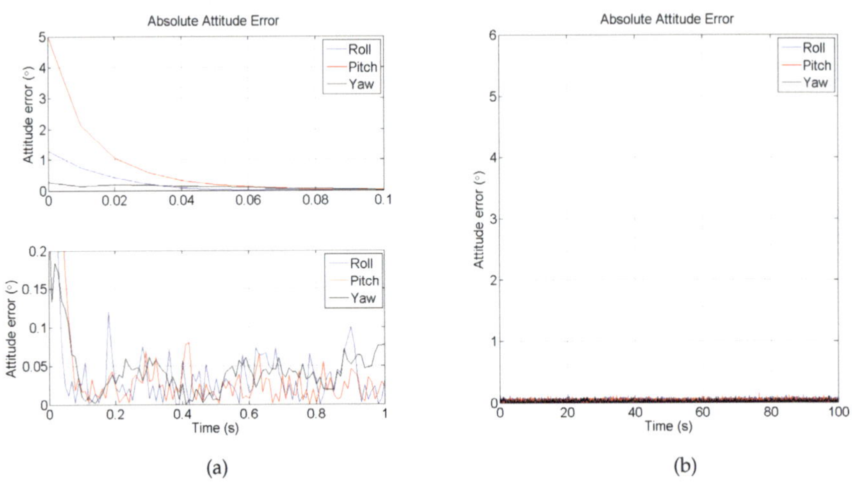

Figure 12.
Absolute attitude error.

	SW	1 PE	2 PE
Total	660	363	272

Table 1.
Overall latency for the single nanosatellite. All values in μs.

initial noisy estimate. The bottom figure shows the first second of the simulation, highlighting the ability of the filter to maintain its accuracy ($< 0.1^{\circ}$ error) after convergence. **Figure 12b** shows that the UKF is able to correct for the inaccuracies arising from the gyroscopic bias and bias drift over the full duration of the simulation.

(a) At the very beginning of the simulation.

(b) For the full simulation.

These results demonstrate that there are no implementation issues when taking the UKF to a HW/SW codesign; the codesign, and IP core, is able to completely replicate software-based implementations of the UKF. The overall latency of the C (SW) implementation and the HW/SW codesign (serial and parallel) for the single nanosatellite case were measured using the ARMv7 Performance Monitoring Unit (PMU) and can be seen in **Table 1**. This overall latency is the time taken to complete one full iteration of the UKF (all steps). The 1 PE case offers a modest $1.8\times$ increase in performance over the C (SW) implementation and can be run at ≈ 2 kHz which is more than adequate for the sampling frequency assumed by the simulation. The 2 PE case offers a slightly better $2.4\times$ speed-up over the C (SW) implementation. Note that the processor system operates at a clock frequency more than six times the frequency used by the IP core (667 vs. 100 MHz), yet the IP core is still able to outperform the C (SW) implementation.

5. Implementation analysis of the hardware/software codesign

Synthesis and implementation runs were targeted at the Zynq-7000 XC7Z045 at a target frequency of 100 MHz. Though the implementations of the example applications presented in Section 4 was for the Zynq-7000 XC7Z020, the codesign does not fit on this device for larger numbers of processing elements. In order to still compare implementation details, this larger device in the Zynq-7000 family is used instead. All the devices in the Zynq-7000 family feature the same processing system; the only difference for larger devices is the amount of programmable logic available.

Resource utilisation of the device by the IP core is reported by Vivado post-implementation. The power analysis is done via the Xilinx Power Estimator (XPE) post-implementation; all power estimates exclude the device static power dissipation and the processing system power draw.

The execution time (latency) for the hardware part is measured via behavioural simulation in Vivado Simulator, assuming a clock frequency of 100 MHz; this assumption was validated post-implementation for all designs. Though behavioural simulations are usually used for only functional verification, Vivado Simulator provides cycle-accurate execution times as long as timing assumptions made in the simulation are verified post-implementation. The entire IP core utilises synchronous logic and is on a single clock domain which makes confirming the proper distribution of the assumed clock signals, in this case 100 MHz, relatively straightforward.

The execution time (latency) of the software part is measured via the ARMv7 Performance Monitoring Unit (PMU), which counts processor clock cycles between two epochs; because the number of processor clock cycles to perform a given task can vary, each measurement was conducted at least 10 times, and the average latency measured is reported here.

5.1 Synthesis results

Synthesis results for a selection of different numbers of processing elements can be seen in **Table 2**. These results do not include the processor but do include the logic necessary for the AXI4 interface ports. The initial numbers of PEs were chosen to be multiples of the number of augmented state variables so that the major datapaths remained data efficient. Recall, for example, the matrix multiply-add datapath (Section 3.2.2); each PE calculates an entire row in the result matrix. If the number of PEs is not a multiple of the size of the matrix, then the last iteration of the calculations will not have enough data to fill all the PEs making the datapath slightly inefficient.

For low numbers of processing elements, the codesign utilises a relatively small percentage of the available resources. The XC7Z045 is a mid-range device in the Zynq-7000 series which means even the 10 PE case still only uses a quarter of the available LUTs. The codesign does not require a proportionally large amount of any one resource; in fact, the design uses a disproportionately smaller amount of FFs than other resources. This will allow easier integration into a full SoC, particularly if partially reconfigurable regions are used. Requiring too much of any one resource type can lead to placement and routing issues since resource on-chip locations are fixed by the manufacturer. This also implies that additional register stages could be added to major datapaths, which would increase the overall latency but could allow an increase in clock frequency as well. If the increase in clock frequency was greater than the increase in latency, the overall performance of the design would benefit.

5.2 Power consumption

A power consumption breakdown for the hardware IP core (i.e. excluding the processor) can be seen in **Table 3**. The power consumption for low numbers of PEs is reasonably low, due to the area efficiency design goals and the heavy utilisation of the FPGA clock that enable resources to disable modules that are not currently in use. For reference, the device static power consumption (@ 25°C) is ≈245 mW, and the rough power consumption of the processing system is ≈1.5 W. A conservative estimate of the electrical power available to a CubeSat is in the order of 1–2 W per unit [15]; larger 2–3 U or more CubeSats have a greater surface area to cover in solar panels. The 1 PE case could be incorporated into a 1 U or larger CubeSat with relative ease, but even for just the 2 PE case, a 2 U CubeSat or larger may be necessary.

Resource	1 PE	2 PE	5 PE	10 PE
FF	7668 (2)	14,286 (3)	27,311 (6)	48,714 (11)
LUT	5764 (3)	15,158 (7)	29,500 (13)	53,427 (24)
BRAM	16.5 (3)	36.5 (7)	62 (11)	109.5 (20)
DSP48	35 (4)	62 (7)	104 (12)	182 (20)

Table 2.
Resource utilisation (% total) on the XC7Z045.

Resource	1 PE	2 PE	5 PE	10 PE
Clocks	38	74	136	234
Signals	24	83	144	261
Logic	23	76	126	219
BRAM	51	82	112	209
DSP	4	6	21	52
Total	140	336	549	975

Table 3.
Power consumption of the codesign. All values in mW.

	SW	1 PE	2 PE	5 PE	10 PE
Sig. gen.	—	—	92	61	51
System model	52	137	137	137	137
Predict	522	170	13	8.5	6.5
Update	87	56	30	21	17
Total	660	363	272	228	212

Table 4.
Latency of each stage for the codesign. System models encompass propagation through both the `predict` *and the* `update` *models on the processor. All values in μs.*

5.3 Timing analysis

A breakdown of the execution time (latency) of different modules can be seen in **Table 4**. The design spends a large amount of the time propagating the sigma points through the two system models. The majority of the time spent by the design is actually in these system models, making the software part the main bottleneck. Looking at the sigma point propagation process a little closer, however, the latency of reading the sigma points from the memory buffer and of writing the transformed points back to the memory buffer was 116 μs. The actual calculation of the system models took a mere 21 μs. So, the bottleneck is actually the speed of the AXI4 port in transferring data between the processor and the memory buffer. Using a higher-performance communication, bus or other techniques such as direct memory access (DMA) ports may alleviate this issue, but intra-chip communication methods are beyond the scope of this chapter.

For the hardware part, the majority of time is spent in the `sig_gen` step. The two modules in the `sig_gen` step, the triangular linear equation solver and the matrix multiply-add, are both large matrix operations which scale with the number of augmented state variables. Operations in the `predict` and `update` steps tend to scale with the number of state or observation variables, respectively, which are always necessarily smaller than the number of augmented state variables. It should be noted that the hardware part appears to suffer from diminishing returns with regard to decreasing the latency as the number of processing elements increases.

6. Conclusion

In this chapter, a scalable FPGA-based implementation of the unscented Kalman filter was presented. The proposed design balances development effort/complexity with performance, combining the advantages of both the traditional software approach and hardware approaches to create a design that system designers can easily use in a potentially wide variety of applications. Simulation and physical implementation results of the codesign were presented. The demonstration application simulated the attitude determination system of an uncontrolled nanosatellite, and the physical implementation was performed on the Xilinx XC7Z045.

Author details

Jeremy Soh and Xiaofeng Wu*
School of Aerospace, Mechanical and Mechatronic Engineering, University of Sydney, Sydney, Australia

*Address all correspondence to: xiaofeng.wu@sydney.edu.au

References

[1] Soh J. A scalable, portable, FPGA-based implementation of the Unscented Kalman Filter. Ph.D. University of Sydney, Feb. 2017. Available from: http://hdl.handle.net/2123/17286

[2] Michell GD, Gupta RK. Hardware/software co-design. In: Proceedings of the IEEE 85.3; Mar. 1997. pp. 349-365. ISSN: 0018-9219. DOI:10.1109/5.558708

[3] Wolf W. A decade of hardware/software codesign. In: Computer 36.4; Apr. 2003. pp. 38-43. ISSN: 0018-9162. DOI: 10.1109/MC.2003.1193227

[4] Teich J. Hardware/software Codesign: The past, the present, and predicting the future. In: Proceedings of the IEEE 100.Special Centennial Issue; May 2012. pp. 1411-1430. ISSN: 0018-9219. DOI: 10.1109/JPROC.2011.2182009

[5] Gelb A. Applied Optimal Estimation. Cambridge, Massachusetts: MIT Press; 1974

[6] Nørgaard M, Poulsen NK, Ravn O. "New developments in state estimation for nonlinear systems". Automatica 36.11 (2000), pp. 1627-1638. ISSN: 0005-1098. DOI: http://dx.doi.org/10.1016/S0005-1098(00)00089-3. URL: http://www.sciencedirect.com/science/article/pii/S0005109800000893

[7] Simon D. Optimal State Estimation: Kalman, H Infinity, and Nonlinear Approaches. Hoboken, New Jersey: John Wiley & Sons; 2006

[8] Crassidis JL, Markley FL, Cheng Y. Survey of nonlinear attitude estimation methods. Journal of Guidance Control and Dynamics. 2007;**30**(1):12

[9] Patwardhan SC, Narasimhan S, Jagadeesan P, Gopaluni B, Shah SL. Nonlinear Bayesian state estimation: A review of recent developments. In: Control Engineering Practice 20.10; 2012. 4th Symposium on Advanced Control of Industrial Processes (ADCONIP). pp. 933-953. ISSN: 0967-0661. DOI: http://dx.doi.org/10.1016/j.conengprac.2012.04.003. URL: http://www.sciencedirect.com/science/article/pii/S0967066112000871

[10] Julier S, Uhlmann J. Unscented filtering and nonlinear estimation. Proceedings of the IEEE. 2004;**92**(3):401-422

[11] Kandepu R, Foss B, Imsland L. "Applying the unscented Kalman filter for nonlinear state estimation". Journal of Process Control 18.7–8 (2008), pp. 753-768. ISSN: 0959-1524. DOI: 10.1016/j.jprocont.2007.11.004. URL: http://www.sciencedirect.com/science/article/pii/S0959152407001655

[12] Julier S. The spherical simplex unscented transformation. American Control Conference, 2003. Proceedings of the 2003. Vol. 3. June 2003. pp. 2430-2434. DOI: 10.1109/ACC.2003.1243439

[13] Golub GH, Van Loan CF. Matrix computations. 3rd ed. Baltimore: Johns Hopkins University Press; 1996

[14] Yang D, Peterson G, Li H, Sun J. An FPGA implementation for solving Least Square problem. In: Field Programmable Custom Computing Machines, 2009. FCCM '09. 17th IEEE Symposium on. Apr. 2009, pp. 303-306. DOI: 10.1109/FCCM.2009.47

[15] Selva D, Krejci D. A survey and assessment of the capabilities of Cubesats for earth observation. Acta Astronautica. 2012;**74**:50-68. ISSN: 0094-5765. DOI: http://dx.doi.org/10.1016/j.actaastro.2011.12.014. URL: http://www.sciencedirect.com/science/article/pii/S0094576511003742

Chapter 6

Novel Direct and Accurate Identification of Kalman Filter for General Systems Described by a Box-Jenkins Model

Rajamani Doraiswami and Lahouari Cheded

Abstract

A novel robust Kalman filter (KF)-based controller is proposed for a multivariable system to accurately track a specified trajectory under unknown stochastic disturbance and measurement noise. The output is a sum of uncorrelated signal, disturbance and measurement noise. The system model is observable but not controllable while the signal one is controllable and observable. An emulator-based two-stage identification is employed to obtain a robust model needed to design the robust controller. The system and KF are identified and the signal and output error estimated. From the identified models, minimal realizations of the signal and KF, the disturbance model and whitening filter are obtained using balanced model reduction techniques. It is shown that the signal model is a transfer matrix relating the system output and the KF residual, and the residual is the whitened output error. The disturbance model is identified by inverse filtering. A feedback-feedforward controller is designed and implemented using an internal model of the reference driven by the error between the reference and the signal estimate, the feedforward of reference and output error. The successful evaluation of the proposed scheme on a simulated autonomously-guided drone gives ample encouragement to test it later, on a real one.

Keywords: identification, Box-Jenkins model, Kalman filter, whitening filter, signal estimation, model reduction, robust controller, feedback controller, feedforward controller, internal model principle, autonomous vehicles, drones

1. Introduction

In conventional Kalman filter applications, the system involved is typically linearized and then identified. Based on the identified system, the Kalman filter is then identified. In this chapter, we propose a novel approach in that (a) the system is represented by a more general model, termed multi-input multi-output Box-Jenkins (MIMO BJ model) which subsumes all previous classical models, such as ARMA models and their derivatives, and (b) the associated Kalman filter identification is carried out directly, i.e. it does not necessitate the prior identification of the system involved. The various tools involved in our proposed approach are all explained below.

1.1 Box-Jenkins model and its applications

Identification of a class of system described by MIMO BJ model, and the associated Kalman filter directly from the input-output data is proposed [1, 2]. There is no need to specify the covariance of the disturbance and the measurement noise, thereby avoiding the use the Riccati equation to solve for the Kalman gain. The output is the desired waveform, termed signal, corrupted by a stochastic disturbance and zero-mean white measurement noise. The state-space BJ model is an augmented system formed of the signal and disturbance model. The signal model and the disturbance models are driven respectively by a user-defined accessible input, and an inaccessible zero-mean white noise process. The signal model is generally a cascade, parallel and feedback combinations of subsystems such as controllers, actuators, plants, and sensors [3]. Unlike the ARMA model, the Box-Jenkins model is observable but not controllable while the signal model is both controllable and observable. In other words, the transfer matrix of the system is non-minimal whereas that of the signal is minimal. This issue will need to be addressed in the identification and implementation of the Kalman filter.

1.2 Kalman filter and its key properties

The structure of the Kalman filter is determined using the internal model principle which establishes the necessary and sufficient condition for the tracking of the output of a dynamical system [3, 4]. In accordance with this principle, the Kalman filter consists of (a) a copy of the system model driven by the residuals, and (b) a gain term, termed the Kalman gain, to stabilize the filter. The Kalman gain is determined such that the residual of the Kalman filter is a zero-mean white noise process with minimum variance. The Kalman filter enjoys the following key properties:

Tracking a signal: The estimate of the Kalman filter tracks a given signal if and only if the model that generates the signals including those of the noise and disturbances is embodied in the Kalman filter. In other words, the Kalman filter tracks the input, thanks to its internal model-based structure [3, 4].

Model matching: The residual is a zero-mean white noise process if and only if there is no mismatch between the actual model of the system and its identified version embodied in the Kalman filter, and its variance is minimum [4].

Optimality: The estimate is optimal in the sense that it is the best estimate that can be obtained by any estimator in the class of all estimators that are constrained by the same assumptions [5].

Robustness: Thanks to the feedback (closed-loop) configuration of the Kalman filter with residual feedback, the Kalman filter provides the highest robustness against the effect of disturbance and model variations [5].

Model-mismatch: If there is a model mismatch, then the residual will not be a zero-mean white noise process and an additive term termed fault-indicative term will occur. The fault-indicative term is a filtered version of the deviation in the linear regression model of the system or that of the signal [6–8].

1.3 Identification using residual model

The equation error in the regression model of the system is a colored noise process, and hence a direct identification of the system model from the input-output data by minimizing the equation error will not ensure that the estimates are consistent, unbiased, and efficient. The fundamental requirement of identification is that the leftover signal from identification, namely the residual is a zero-mean white noise process that contains no information. To meet this requirement, both the input and output of the system are filtered. Among the class of all linear whitening filters, the Kalman filter is the best. The system model is indirectly identified by minimizing the residual generated by the Kalman filter instead of the equation error. The Subspace Method (SM) uses the structure of the state-space model of the Kalman filter, whereas the prediction error method (PEM), which is the gold standard in system identification, is developed from the residual model [1, 9–11].

1.4 Emulator-based two-stage identification

The static and dynamic behavior of a physical system change as a result of variations in the parameters of some of its subsystems such as sensors, actuators, plant, disturbance models, and controllers. As the parameters of these subsystems are not generally accessible to generate data, instead, emulators, which are hardware or software devices, are connected in cascade to the output, input or both, of the subsystems. An emulator is a transfer function block which mimics the variations in the associated subsystems including the disturbance model. An emulator takes the form of a static gain or an all-pass filter to induce gain or phase variations in the subsystem it is connected to. Emulator parameters are perturbed to mimic various normal and abnormal, or faulty, operating scenarios resulting from variations in these subsystems. The emulator-generated data is employed in (a) the identification of robust systems and signal models and their associated Kalman filters using the two-stage identification scheme [2, 3, 6–8].

A two-stage identification is used in various applications including the non-parametric identification of impulse response, estimation of Markov parameters in the SM, in model predictive control, identification of a signal model and in system identification. The use of the two-stage identification is inspired by the seminal paper by [12] for an accurate estimation of the parameters of an impulse response from measurements in an additive white noise. It is shown via simulation that the variance of the parameter estimation error approaches the Cramer-Rao lower bound [13]. Further, it is shown analytically that using a high-order model (with an order several times larger than the true order) improves significantly the accuracy of the parameter estimates. The two-stage scheme has not received much attention in system identification although it has been mentioned as an alternative scheme to the PEM [1, 14], and has been successfully employed in identification in [15–17].

It should be emphasized that the prediction error method (PEM), viewed as a gold standard for system identification, is not geared for the estimation of the signal buried in the output, i.e. it is developed for the ARMA model and not for the Box-Jenkins one. A two-stage identification of the Box-Jenkins model is proposed as the system model is observable but not controllable while the signal model is both controllable and observable:

- In the first stage, the robust system model and the associated Kalman filter are identified using the emulator-generated data using PEM, and the signal and the output error are both estimated. Further, the whitening filter that relates the output error and the residual is obtained.

- In the second stage, minimal realizations of the signal model and the associated Kalman filter are obtained using model reduction method [18].

The high- order for the first stage and the reduced-order for the second are both selected using the Akaike information criterion (AIC) and are cross-checked by verifying the whiteness of the associated residual. The two-stage identification has also been successfully employed in the identification model.

The question arises as to how to obtain the system model and the signal model from the identified high-order model Kalman filters. A key property of the Kalman filter is established here, namely that the transfer matrix of the signal and the system is the matrix fraction description model derived from the Kalman filter residual model of the system. This property is exploited to derive the signal and the system transfer matrices. The state-space models of the signal and the system models are derived from the identified state-space models of the Kalman filters. Thus, the proposed scheme identifies (a) the Kalman filter for the system, (b) the Kalman filter for the signal first. Then, the system model and the signal model are separately obtained.

The proposed scheme is further extended to identify the signal model to complement the PEM. In the first stage, a very high-order model is identified using PEM. In the second stage, the signal model is identified using a balanced model reduction of the high-order identified model obtained in the first stage. The PEM and state-space method (SM) are both tailored to identify the signal model and estimate the signal by employing the proposed version of the two-stage identification scheme. The results of the comparison of the performance of these methods in identifying the system and signal models are presented.

1.5 Highlights of the contributions

- The Auto-Regressive (AR), The Moving Average (MA), and the Auto-Regressive and Moving Average (ARMA) models are all special cases of the proposed Box-Jenkins model. As this model is more general and hence has wider applications, including robust controller design; estimation of latent variables; monitoring of the status of the system, fault diagnosis, development of condition-based maintenance programs and design of fault-tolerant systems; filtering of signals, speech enhancement, noise and echo cancelation in communication; 2-D image filtering and tracking of moving objects.

- The state-space models of the system and the signal models are derived from the identified Kalman filters, by invoking the (causal) invertibility of the output error and the residual [5].

- An efficient scheme to monitor the status of the system may be implemented from the proposed scheme. First the status of the system is monitored by analyzing the residual of the Kalman filter of the system model. If there is a variation, then the residual of the Kalman filter of the signal model is analyzed to ascertain whether a fault has occurred.

- In practice, disturbances are inevitable, and can negatively affect the system performance. When the system is in an abnormal state, it is not in general easy to determine whether the abnormal operation is the result of variations in the disturbance or the occurrence of a fault. The proposed scheme provides a simple solution by analyzing the residuals of both Kalman filters as the residual of the Kalman filter for the system captures the variations in both the system and disturbance models, while that of the Kalman filter for the signal, and captures only the variations in the signal model. This is crucial for reducing false alarm, and all its concomitant risks and costs, resulting from variations in the disturbance and not in the signal model [19].

- The PEM (SM) may be tailored to identify the signal model and estimate the signal itself by using the proposed two-stage identification scheme.

1.6 Applications

Applications include monitoring the status of the system and the signal models, distinguishing between the variations in the disturbance model and those in the signal model to help diagnose a fault in the system and ensure a low false alarm probability, estimating the latent variable, namely the signal, developing a framework for applications including robust controller design; fault diagnosis; speech and biological signal processing; tracking of moving objects, design of soft sensors to replace maintenance-prone hardware sensors, evaluate and monitor product quality, meeting the ever-increasing need for fault-tolerant systems for mission-critical systems found in aerospace, the nuclear power systems, and autonomous vehicles.

2. Problem formulation

The output $\boldsymbol{y}(k) \in \mathbb{R}^q$ is an additive sum of the signal $\boldsymbol{s}(k) \in \mathbb{R}^q$, disturbance, $\boldsymbol{d}(k) \in \mathbb{R}^q$and the measurement noise $\boldsymbol{v}(k) \in \mathbb{R}^q$ where $\mathbb{R}$ is real scalar field.

$$\boldsymbol{y}(k) = \boldsymbol{s}(k) + \boldsymbol{d}(k) + \boldsymbol{v}(k) \tag{1}$$

Where the signal and the disturbance models are:

$$\boldsymbol{s}(z) = \boldsymbol{G}_s(z)\boldsymbol{u}(z) \tag{2}$$

$$\boldsymbol{d}(z) = \boldsymbol{G}_w(z)\boldsymbol{w}(z) \tag{3}$$

Where $\boldsymbol{u}(k) \in \mathbb{R}^q$ is the input; $\boldsymbol{w}(k) \in \mathbb{R}^p$ is zero-mean white noise process that generates the disturbance $\boldsymbol{d}(k) \in \mathbb{R}^p$, and is uncorrelated with the measurement noise $\boldsymbol{v}(k)$; $\boldsymbol{G}_s(z) = D_s^{-1}(z)\boldsymbol{N}_s(z)$ and $\boldsymbol{G}_w(z) = D_w^{-1}(z)\boldsymbol{N}_w(z)$ are qxp transfer matrix of order n_s and n_w respectively; $\boldsymbol{\vartheta}(k)=\boldsymbol{d}(k) + \boldsymbol{v}(k)$ is the *output error*.

The signal model $\boldsymbol{G}_s(z)$ is formed of cascade and parallel combinations of the subsystems such as actuators, plant and the sensors. Let the state space model of the signal and the disturbance models be respectively $(\boldsymbol{A}_s, \boldsymbol{B}_s, \boldsymbol{C}_s)$ and $(\boldsymbol{A}_w, \boldsymbol{B}_w, \boldsymbol{C}_w)$.

Figure 1 shows the input-output model relating the input, the signal model, the signal, the disturbance model, the disturbance, the measurement noise and the output.

Linear regression model:

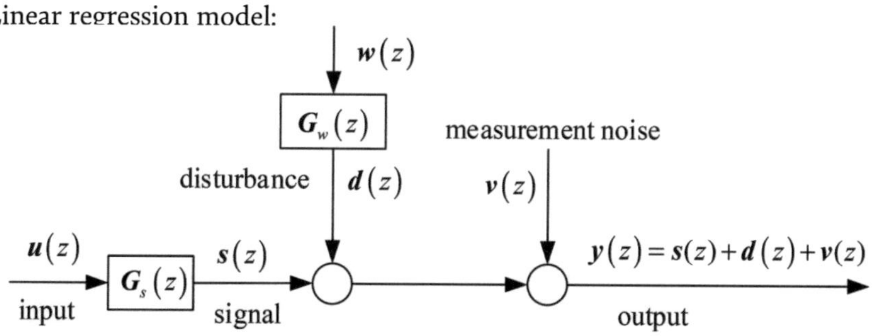

Figure 1.
System: signal, the disturbance and the measurement noise.

Using, (1)–(3), the expression for the linear regression becomes:

$$\begin{aligned} D_{sw}(z)\boldsymbol{y}(z) &= D_w(z)\boldsymbol{N}_{sw}(z)\boldsymbol{u}(z) + \boldsymbol{\upsilon}(z) \\ \boldsymbol{\upsilon}(z) &= D_s(z)\boldsymbol{N}_w(z)\boldsymbol{w}(z) + D_{sw}(z)\boldsymbol{v}(z) \end{aligned} \tag{4}$$

Where $\boldsymbol{\upsilon}(z) = D(z)\boldsymbol{\vartheta}(z)$ is the equation error; $D_{sw}(z) = D_s(z)D_w(z)$ and $\boldsymbol{N}_{sw}(z) = D_w(z)\boldsymbol{N}_s(z)$ are respectively the denominator and numerator polynomials. The model is termed Box-Jenkins model.

Note that the model that generates the equation error $\boldsymbol{\upsilon}(z)$ is a Moving Average (MA) model, whereas the one that generates the output error $\boldsymbol{\vartheta}(k)$ is an Auto-Regressive Moving-Average (ARMA) model.

Augmented state-space model: The augmented state-space representation of the multi-input and multi-output (MIMO) system $(\boldsymbol{A}, \boldsymbol{B}, \boldsymbol{C}, \boldsymbol{D})$ formed of the signal model $(\boldsymbol{A}_s, \boldsymbol{B}_s, \boldsymbol{C}_s, \boldsymbol{D}_s)$ and $(\boldsymbol{A}_w, \boldsymbol{B}_w, \boldsymbol{C}_w, \boldsymbol{D}_w)$ representing a p-input, q-output system, is given by:

$$\begin{aligned} \boldsymbol{x}(k+1) &= \boldsymbol{A}\boldsymbol{x}(k) + \boldsymbol{B}\boldsymbol{u}(k) + \boldsymbol{E}_w\boldsymbol{w}(k) \\ \boldsymbol{s}(k) &= \boldsymbol{C}_s\boldsymbol{x}(k) + \boldsymbol{D}_s\boldsymbol{u}(k) \\ \boldsymbol{y}(k) &= \boldsymbol{C}\boldsymbol{x}(k) + \boldsymbol{D}\boldsymbol{u}(k) + \boldsymbol{v}(k) \end{aligned} \tag{5}$$

Where $A = \begin{bmatrix} \boldsymbol{A}_s & \boldsymbol{0} \\ \boldsymbol{0} & \boldsymbol{A}_w \end{bmatrix}; B = \begin{bmatrix} \boldsymbol{B}_s \\ \boldsymbol{0} \end{bmatrix}; \boldsymbol{E}_w = \begin{bmatrix} \boldsymbol{0} \\ \boldsymbol{B}_w \end{bmatrix}; C = [C_s \;\; C_w];$ $\boldsymbol{A} \in \mathbb{R}^{nxn}$ is an augmented state transition matrix formed of $\boldsymbol{A}_s \in \Re^{n_s x n_s}$ and $\boldsymbol{A}_w \in \Re^{n_w x n_w}$;

$\boldsymbol{B} = \begin{bmatrix} \boldsymbol{B}_1 \, \boldsymbol{B}_2 \, . \, \boldsymbol{B}_p \end{bmatrix} \in \mathbb{R}^{nxp}$; $\boldsymbol{C} = \begin{bmatrix} \boldsymbol{C}_1 \, \boldsymbol{C}_2 \, . \, \boldsymbol{C}_q \end{bmatrix}^T \in \mathbb{R}^{qxn}$; $\boldsymbol{E}_w \in \mathbb{R}^{nxp}$ is a disturbance entry matrix;

$\boldsymbol{x}(k) = [x_1(k) \quad x_2(k) \quad x_3(k) \quad \ldots \quad x_n(k)]^T \in \mathbb{R}^n$; $\boldsymbol{s}(k) = [s_1(k) \quad s_2(k) \quad s_3(k) \ldots s_q(k)]^T \in \mathbb{R}^q$;

$\boldsymbol{u}(k) = \begin{bmatrix} u_1(k) \, u_2(k) \, u_3(k) \ldots u_p(k) \end{bmatrix}^T \in \mathbb{R}^p$;

$\boldsymbol{y}(k) = \begin{bmatrix} y_1(k) \, y_2(k) \, y_3(k) \ldots y_q(k) \end{bmatrix}^T \in \mathbb{R}^q$ are respectively the state, the input and output; $n = n_s + n_w$ is the order; $\boldsymbol{w}(k) \in \mathbb{R}^n$ and $\boldsymbol{v}(k) \in \mathbb{R}^q$ are respectively the disturbances and measurement noise; $D_{sw}(z) = |(z\boldsymbol{I} - \boldsymbol{A}_s)||(z\boldsymbol{I} - \boldsymbol{A}_w)|$ where $|(.)|$ is the determinant of $(.)$. Using $D_{sw}(z) = D_s(z)D_w(z)$ and $\boldsymbol{N}_{sw}(z) = D_w(z)\boldsymbol{N}_s(z)$ we get:

$$\begin{aligned} \boldsymbol{G}(z) &= \boldsymbol{C}(z\boldsymbol{I} - \boldsymbol{A})^{-1}\boldsymbol{B} + \boldsymbol{D} = D_{sw}^{-1}(z)\boldsymbol{N}_{sw}(z) \\ \boldsymbol{G}(z) &= D_s^{-1}(z)\boldsymbol{N}_s(z) = \boldsymbol{G}_s(z) \end{aligned} \tag{6}$$

The augmented transfer matrix is not a minimal realization of the system output model as there is (stable) pole-zero cancelation since the polynomial $D_w(z)$, which is common to both the numerator $\boldsymbol{N}_{sw}(z)$ and the denominator $D_{sw}(z)$. In other words, $\boldsymbol{N}_{sw}(z)$ and $D_{sw}(z)$ are not coprime. The signal model $(\boldsymbol{A}_s, \boldsymbol{B}_s, \boldsymbol{C}_s, \boldsymbol{D}_s)$ associated with signal model $\boldsymbol{G}_s(z)$ is controllable and observable while $(\boldsymbol{A}, \boldsymbol{B}, \boldsymbol{C}, \boldsymbol{D})$, associated with$\boldsymbol{G}(z)$, is merely an observable. $(\boldsymbol{A}_s, \boldsymbol{B}_s, \boldsymbol{C}_s, \boldsymbol{D}_s)$ $(\boldsymbol{G}_s(z))$ is a minimal realization of $(\boldsymbol{A}, \boldsymbol{B}, \boldsymbol{C}, \boldsymbol{D})$ $(\boldsymbol{G}(z))$.

Assumptions: It is assumed that (a) the disturbance $\boldsymbol{w}(k)$ and the measurement noise$\boldsymbol{v}(k)$ are independent zero-mean Gaussian white noise processes with *unknown* but finite covariance, $\boldsymbol{Q} = E\left[\boldsymbol{w}(k)\boldsymbol{w}^T(k)\right]$ and $\boldsymbol{R} = E\left[\boldsymbol{v}(k)\boldsymbol{v}^T(k)\right]$, respectively, and are inaccessible, (b) $(\boldsymbol{A}, \boldsymbol{C})$ is observable, (c) the signal and disturbance models are both minimal, $(\boldsymbol{A}_s, \boldsymbol{B}_s, \boldsymbol{C}_s, \boldsymbol{D}_s)$ and $(\boldsymbol{A}_w, \boldsymbol{B}_w, \boldsymbol{C}_w, \boldsymbol{D}_w)$ are both controllable and observable, (d) The initial conditions $\boldsymbol{x}(0)$, $\boldsymbol{w}(k)$ and $\boldsymbol{v}(k)$ are mutually uncorrelated. However, the signal $\boldsymbol{s}(z)$ and the disturbance $\boldsymbol{w}(z)$ may have spectral overlap, (e) the output error is bounded.

2.1 Kalman filter

Predictor form: A robust Kalman filter of the identified system $(\boldsymbol{A}^0, \boldsymbol{B}^0, \boldsymbol{C}^0, \boldsymbol{D}^0)$ relating the system input $\boldsymbol{u}(z)$ and system output $\boldsymbol{y}(k)$ to the estimated output $\hat{\boldsymbol{y}}(k)$ is:

$$\begin{aligned}\hat{\boldsymbol{x}}(k+1) &= (\boldsymbol{A}^0 - \boldsymbol{K}^0\boldsymbol{C}^0)\hat{\boldsymbol{x}}(k) + (\boldsymbol{B}^0 - \boldsymbol{K}^0\boldsymbol{D}^0)\,\boldsymbol{u}(k) + \boldsymbol{K}^0\boldsymbol{y}(k) \\ \hat{\boldsymbol{y}}(k) &= \boldsymbol{C}^0\hat{\boldsymbol{x}}(k) + \boldsymbol{D}^0\boldsymbol{u}(k) \\ \boldsymbol{e}(k) &= \boldsymbol{y}(k) - \hat{\boldsymbol{y}}(k)\end{aligned} \tag{7}$$

Where $\hat{\boldsymbol{x}}(k) = [\hat{x}_1(k)\hat{x}_2(k)\hat{x}_3(k)...\hat{x}_n(k)]^T \in \mathbb{R}^n$ and $\hat{\boldsymbol{y}}(k) = \left[\hat{y}_1(k)\hat{y}_2(k)\hat{y}_3(k)...\hat{y}_q(k)\right]^T \in \mathbb{R}^q$ are respectively the best estimate of the state $\boldsymbol{x}(k)$, and of the output $\boldsymbol{y}(k)$; $\boldsymbol{e}(k) = \left[e_1(k) \quad e_2(k) \quad e_3(k) \quad ... \quad e_q(k)\right]^T \in \mathbb{R}^q$ is the residual or the innovation sequence; the Kalman gain $\boldsymbol{K}^0 \in \mathbb{R}^{nxq}$ ensures the asymptotic stability of the Kalman filter, i.e. $(\boldsymbol{A}^0 - \boldsymbol{K}^0\boldsymbol{C}^0)$ is strictly Hurwitz having all its eigenvalues strictly inside the unit circle.

Innovation form: There is duality between the predictor, and the innovation forms of the Kalman filter [5]. The output $\boldsymbol{y}(k)$ and the residual $\boldsymbol{e}(k)$ are (causally) invertible. In other words, $\boldsymbol{e}(k)$ can be generated from the output $\boldsymbol{y}(k)$ and $\boldsymbol{r}(k)$ using the (causal) predictor form, and $\boldsymbol{y}(k)$ can be generated from $\boldsymbol{e}(k)$ and $\boldsymbol{r}(k)$ using the innovation form. The Kalman filter given by (7) is termed the predictor form and can be expressed in an alternative form, termed the innovation form, given by:

$$\begin{aligned}\hat{\boldsymbol{x}}(k+1) &= \boldsymbol{A}^0\hat{\boldsymbol{x}}(k) + \boldsymbol{B}^0\boldsymbol{u}(k) + \boldsymbol{K}^0\boldsymbol{e}(k) \\ \hat{\boldsymbol{y}}(k) &= \boldsymbol{C}^0\hat{\boldsymbol{x}}(k) + \boldsymbol{D}^0\boldsymbol{u}(k)\end{aligned} \tag{8}$$

Figure 2 shows the system and the Kalman filter which embodies the system model $(\boldsymbol{A}, \boldsymbol{B}, \boldsymbol{C})$. The inputs to the Kalman filter are the input $\boldsymbol{r}(k)$ and the output $\boldsymbol{y}(k)$which is corrupted by the noise $\boldsymbol{v}(k)$ and affected by the disturbance $\boldsymbol{w}(k)$.

2.2 Residual model

The frequency-domain expression relating the input $\boldsymbol{u}(z) \in \mathbb{R}^p$ and the output $\boldsymbol{y}(z) \in \mathbb{R}^q$ to the residual $\boldsymbol{e}(z) \in \mathbb{R}^q$ is given by the following model termed the *residual model*:

$$\boldsymbol{e}(z) = F^{-1}(z)\overline{\boldsymbol{D}}(z)\boldsymbol{y}(z) - F^{-1}(z)\overline{\boldsymbol{N}}(z)\boldsymbol{u}(z) \tag{9}$$

where $\overline{\boldsymbol{D}}(z)$ and $\overline{\boldsymbol{N}}(z)$ are matrix polynomials, $F(z)$ is the scalar characteristic polynomial termed *Kalman polynomial*, $F(z) = |z\boldsymbol{I} - \boldsymbol{A}^0 + \boldsymbol{K}^0\boldsymbol{C}^0|$;
$D(z) = |(z\boldsymbol{I} - \boldsymbol{A}^0)|$; $\overline{\boldsymbol{D}}(z) = F(z)\left(\boldsymbol{I} - \boldsymbol{C}^0(z\boldsymbol{I} - \boldsymbol{A}^0 + \boldsymbol{K}^0\boldsymbol{C}^0)^{-1}\boldsymbol{K}^0\right)$ is qxq matrix;
$\overline{\boldsymbol{N}}(z) = F(z)\left(\boldsymbol{C}^0(z\boldsymbol{I} - \boldsymbol{A}^0 + \boldsymbol{K}^0\boldsymbol{C}^0)^{-1}(\boldsymbol{B}^0 - \boldsymbol{K}^0\boldsymbol{D}^0) + \boldsymbol{D}^0\right)$ is qxp matrix; $\boldsymbol{I} \in \mathbb{R}^{qxq}$ is an identity matrix;

$$\overline{D}(z) = \begin{bmatrix} \overline{D}_1(z) \\ \overline{D}_2(z) \\ . \\ \overline{D}_q(z) \end{bmatrix} = \begin{bmatrix} \overline{D}_{11}(z) & \overline{D}_{12}(z) & . & \overline{D}_{1q}(z) \\ \overline{D}_{21}(z) & \overline{D}_{22}(z) & . & \overline{D}_{2q}(z) \\ . & ; & . & . \\ \overline{D}_{q1}(z) & \overline{D}_{q2}(z) & . & \overline{D}_{qq}(z) \end{bmatrix};$$
$$\overline{N}(z) = \begin{bmatrix} \overline{N}_1(z) \\ \overline{N}_2(z) \\ . \\ \overline{N}_q(z) \end{bmatrix} = \begin{bmatrix} \overline{N}_{11}(z) & \overline{N}_{12}(z) & . & \overline{N}_{1p}(z) \\ \overline{N}_{21}(z) & \overline{N}_{22}(z) & . & \overline{N}_{2p}(z) \\ . & ; & . & . \\ \overline{N}_{q1}(z) & \overline{N}_{q2}(z) & . & \overline{N}_{qp}(z) \end{bmatrix} \tag{10}$$

$\overline{D}_{ij}(z) = \sum_{\ell=0}^{n} \overline{a}_{ij\ell} z^{-\ell}$; $\overline{N}_{ij}(z) = \sum_{\ell=1}^{n} \overline{b}_{ij\ell} z^{-\ell}$; $\overline{a}_{ij\ell}$ and $\overline{b}_{ij\ell}$ are the coefficients of the polynomials $\overline{D}_{ij}(z)$ and $\overline{N}_{ij}(z)$, respectively. The rational polynomials $F^{-1}(z)\overline{\boldsymbol{D}}(z)$ and $F^{-1}(z)\overline{\boldsymbol{N}}(z)$ associated with the system output $\boldsymbol{y}(z)$ and the input $\boldsymbol{u}(z)$ are termed as an *output IIR filter*, and an *input IIR filter*, respectively. The estimate of the Kalman filter $\hat{\boldsymbol{y}}(k)$ is:

$$\hat{\boldsymbol{y}}(z) = \left(\boldsymbol{I} - F^{-1}(z)\overline{\boldsymbol{D}}(z)\right)\boldsymbol{y}(z) + F^{-1}(z)\overline{\boldsymbol{N}}(z)\boldsymbol{u}(z) \tag{11}$$

The residual model of the Kalman filter forms the backbone of the proposed identification scheme.

2.3 The key properties of the Kalman filter

The map relating the signal and its model, and the output IIR filter and an input IIR filter of residual model is developed next.

The following lemmas are developed by invoking the key property namely that the residual is a zero-mean white noise process if and only if there is no mismatch between the actual model of the system and its identified model embodied in the Kalman filter [4], that is, the identified model embodied in the Kalman filter is identical to that of the actual model:

2.3.1 Derivation of the signal and the signal model

The following Lemma 1 shows that (a) the estimate of the signal model is the matrix fraction description relating the transfer matrices relating the residual of the

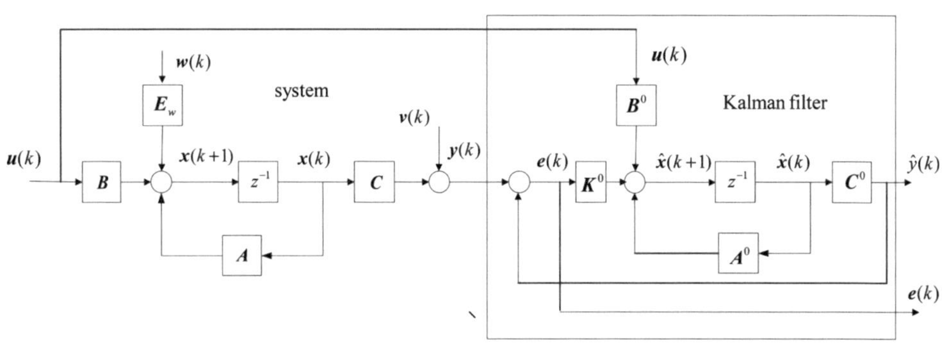

Figure 2.
The system and the Kalman filter model.

Kalman filter to the input, and the output of the system; (b) the estimate of the signal is its output generated by the system input; and the Kalman filter whitens the output error.

Lemma 1

(a) The left-matrix description of the MIMO signal model derived from the state-space model $(\boldsymbol{A}_s^0, \boldsymbol{B}_s^0, \boldsymbol{C}_s^0, \boldsymbol{D}_s^0)$, namely, $\boldsymbol{G}_s(z) = \boldsymbol{C}_s^0 (z\boldsymbol{I} - \boldsymbol{A}_s^0)^{-1} \boldsymbol{B}_s^0 = D_s^{-1}(z)\boldsymbol{N}_s(z)$ and the left-matrix description of the Kalman filter derived from the residual model, $\overline{\boldsymbol{G}}(z) = \overline{\boldsymbol{D}}^{-1}(z)\overline{\boldsymbol{N}}(z)$ are identical. The signal model $\boldsymbol{G}_s(z)$ and the signal $\boldsymbol{s}(z)$ are:

$$\begin{aligned}\hat{\boldsymbol{G}}_s(z) &= \hat{\boldsymbol{G}}(z) = \overline{\boldsymbol{G}}(z) \\ \hat{\boldsymbol{s}}(z) &= \hat{\boldsymbol{G}}_s(z)\boldsymbol{u}(z) = \overline{\boldsymbol{G}}(z)\boldsymbol{u}(z)\end{aligned} \tag{12}$$

Proof:

(a) Consider the residual model (9). Substituting for $\boldsymbol{y}(z)$ yields:

$$F^{-1}(z)\overline{\boldsymbol{D}}(z)\left(D_s^{-1}(z)\boldsymbol{N}_s(z)\boldsymbol{u}(z) - \overline{\boldsymbol{D}}^{-1}(z)\overline{\boldsymbol{N}}(z)\boldsymbol{u}(z) + \boldsymbol{\vartheta}(z)\right) = \boldsymbol{e}(z) \tag{13}$$

Since the residual is a zero-mean, white noise process and is uncorrelated with $\boldsymbol{u}(z)$ and $\boldsymbol{v}(z)$, correlating both sides with the input $\boldsymbol{u}(z^{-1})$ yields:

$$\left(F^{-1}(z)\overline{\boldsymbol{D}}(z)\hat{D}_s^{-1}(z)\hat{\boldsymbol{N}}_s(z) - F^{-1}(z)\overline{\boldsymbol{N}}(z)\right)E\left[\boldsymbol{u}(z)\boldsymbol{u}(z^{-1})\right] = 0 \tag{14}$$

Assuming that the input correlation is not identically equal to zero, i.e. $E[\boldsymbol{u}(z)\boldsymbol{u}(z^{-1})] \neq \boldsymbol{0}$ yields:

$$\left(F^{-1}(z)\overline{\boldsymbol{D}}(z)\hat{D}_s^{-1}(z)\hat{\boldsymbol{N}}_s(z) - F^{-1}(z)\overline{\boldsymbol{N}}(z)\right) = 0 \tag{15}$$

Simplifying we get:

$$\hat{D}_s^{-1}(z)\hat{\boldsymbol{N}}_s(z) = \overline{\boldsymbol{D}}^{-1}(z)\overline{\boldsymbol{N}}(z) \tag{16}$$

Hence $\hat{\boldsymbol{G}}_s(z) = \overline{\boldsymbol{G}}(z)$ holds. Since $D_{sw}(z) = D_s(z)D_w(z)$ and $\boldsymbol{N}_{sw}(z) = D_w(z)\boldsymbol{N}_s(z)$ are not coprime as $D_w(z)$ is a common factor, then $\hat{\boldsymbol{G}}_s(z) = \hat{\boldsymbol{G}}(z) = \overline{\boldsymbol{G}}(z)$.

(b) Substituting (16) in (13) we get

$$\boldsymbol{e}(z) = F^{-1}(z)\overline{\boldsymbol{D}}(z)\boldsymbol{\vartheta}(z) = F^{-1}(z)D^{-1}(z)\overline{\boldsymbol{D}}(z)\boldsymbol{v}(z) \tag{17}$$

where $F^{-1}(z)\overline{\boldsymbol{D}}(z) = \left(\boldsymbol{I} - \boldsymbol{C}(z\boldsymbol{I} - \boldsymbol{A} + \boldsymbol{K}\boldsymbol{C})^{-1}\boldsymbol{K}\right)$.

Proof:

follows from $\boldsymbol{\vartheta}(k) = \boldsymbol{d}(k) + \boldsymbol{v}(k)$, (9) and

2.3.2 Derivation of the output error and its model

The following Lemma 2 shows that the output error is the difference between the output and the estimate of the signal; the estimate of the output error model is the matrix fraction description of the transfer matrices relating the residual of the Kalman filter to the input; the estimate of the output error is obtained as its output when its input is the residual. It is assumed that the transfer matrix of the Kalman filter $F^{-1}(z)\overline{D}(z) = \left(I - C^0\left(zI - A^0 + K^0C^0\right)^{-1}K^0\right)$ relating the output $y(z)$ and the residual $e(z)$ is minimum-phase, that is both the numerator and the denominator polynomials are asymptotically stable.

Lemma 2.
If the matrix $\overline{D}(z)$is invertible, the output error $\vartheta(z) = d(z) + v(z)$ is given by:

$$\begin{aligned} \hat{\vartheta}(k) &= y(k) - \hat{s}(k) \\ \hat{\vartheta}(z) &= F(z)\overline{D}^{-1}(z)e(z) \end{aligned} \tag{18}$$

where $F(z)\overline{D}^{-1}(z) = \left(I - C^0\left(zI - A^0 + K^0C^0\right)^{-1}K^0\right)^{-1}$ is termed the disturbance model estimate which generates the output error when excited by the residual.

Proof:
Using (17) we get (18).

As the input $w(k)$ driving the disturbance model is not accessible, then by substituting the actual input $w(k)$ by the residual $e(k)$, although both are zero-mean white noise processes, only the denominator polynomial of the disturbance model can be identified. Hence the term "disturbance model estimate".

Minimum realization of the output error model is obtained using balanced model reduction method by treating $e(z)$ as the input and $\hat{\vartheta}(k)$ as the output of a model [7].

2.3.3 Minimal realization of the signal model

There are two approaches to identifying the signal model and the signal. One approach is by deriving them from the residual model of the Kalman filter as shown in Lemma 1 given by (12) and the other approach is to invoke the duality between the predictor form (7) and the innovation form (8) of the Kalman filter. The latter approach may be more convenient.

In view of (12), the system model $G(z)$ and the signal model $G_s(z)$ is derived from the identified Kalman filter (7) by simply replacing the transition matrix of the Kalman filter $A^0 - K^0C^0$ by the system transition matrixA^0.

Lemma 3.

$$\begin{aligned} \left(A^0, B^0, C^0, D^0\right) &= \left(A^0 + K^0C^0, B^0, C^0, D^=\right) \\ \left(A_s, B_s, C_s, D_s\right) &= minreal\left(A^0, B^0, C^0, D^0\right) \end{aligned} \tag{19}$$

Where $minreal\left(A^0, B^0, C^0, D^0\right)$ is the minimal realization of $\left(A^0, B^0, C^0, D^0\right)$.

Proof

There is duality between the predictor form (7) and the innovation form (8) of the Kalman filter [5]. The output $y(k)$and the residual $e(k)$ are (causally) invertible. In other words, $e(k)$ can be generated from the output $y(k)$ and $r(k)$ using the (causally) predictor form, and $y(k)$ can be generated from $e(k)$ and $r(k)$ using the innovation form [3]. Moreover, $\left(A^0, B^0, C^0, D^0\right)$ and $\left(A_s^0, B_s^0, C_s^0, D_s^0\right)$ are associated with the system transfer matrices $G(z) = D^{-1}(z)N(z)$ and

$G_s(z) = D_s^{-1}(z)N_s(z)$ respectively, as shown in (4), implying that $(A_s^0, B_s^0, C_s^0, D_s^0)$ is a minimum realization of (A^0, B^0, C^0, D^0).

The minimum realization of the system $(A_s^0, B_s^0, C_s^0, D_s^0)$ is obtained from the balanced model reduction method by treating $u(k)$ as the input and $\hat{s}(k)$ as the output of a model [7].

3. Emulator-based two-stage identification

An identified model at each operating point characterizes the behavior of the system in the neighborhood of that point. In practice, however, the system model may be perturbed because of variations in the parameters of that system. To overcome this problem, the system model is identified by performing a number of emulator parameter-perturbed experiments proposed in [7–9]. Each experiment consists of perturbing one or more emulator parameters. A robust model is identified as the best fit to the input–output data from the set of emulated perturbations. The robust model thus obtained characterizes the behavior of the system over wider operating regions (in the neighborhood of the operating point) whereas the conventional model characterizes the behavior merely at the nominal operating point (that is, the conventional approach assumes that the model of the system remains unperturbed at every operating point). In [7–9], it is theoretically shown that the identification errors resulting from the variations in the emulator parameters are significantly lower compared to those of the conventional ones based on performing a single experiment (that is, without using emulators). The emulator-based identification scheme is inspired from the model-free artificial neural network approach which captures the static and dynamic behaviors by presenting the neural network with data covering likely operating scenarios. The PEM identifies the robust model of the plant, and the Kalman filter associated with the plant is then derived from the identified model without any a-priori knowledge of the statistics, such as covariance of the disturbance and measurement noise affecting the input-output data.

An accurate emulator-based model identification scheme is proposed and employed here. An emulator, which is modeled as a product of first-order all-pass filters and which induces phase and gain changes, is connected in cascade to the input, output or both, of the signal model to emulate a set of likely operating regimes around the nominal operating point. The identified model is obtained as the best fit over all emulated operating regions, thereby ensuring both accuracy and robustness of the identified model.

3.1 Two-stage identification

- In the first stage, a robust model of the system (A^0, B^0, C^0, D^0) and its associated Kalman filter $(A^0 - K^0C^0, [(B^0 - K^0D^0)\ K^0], C^0, D^0)$ are identified using PEM from the set of the emulator-generated input-output data. Then the estimate $s^0(k)$ of the signal $s(k)$ and the estimate $\hat{\vartheta}(k)$ of the output error $\vartheta(k)$ are derived.

- In the second stage, using the key properties established in Lemmas 1–3, the robust signal model $(A_s^0, B_s^0, C_s^0, D_s^0)$ and its associated Kalman filter $(A_s^0 - K_s^0C_s^0, [B_s^0 - K_s^0D_s^0\ K_s^0], C_s^0, D_s^0)$ are obtained using balanced model reduction method and the PEM.

Akaike Information Criterion: To select an appropriate order for the identified system model in the first stage, and for the signal model in the second stage, the widely popular Akaike Information Criterion (AIC) is used, which weights both the parameter estimation error and the complexity of the model so as to arrive at an optimal order [1].

3.2 Signal model and the Kalman filter

Similar to the Kalman filter for the system (7), the Kalman filter for the signal is:

$$\begin{aligned}\hat{\boldsymbol{x}}_s(k+1) &= \left(\boldsymbol{A}_s^0 - \boldsymbol{K}_s^0\boldsymbol{C}_s^0\right)\hat{\boldsymbol{x}}_s(k) + \left(\boldsymbol{B}_s^0 - \boldsymbol{K}_s^0\boldsymbol{D}_s^0\right)\boldsymbol{u}(k) + \boldsymbol{K}_s^0\boldsymbol{s}^0(k)\\ \hat{\boldsymbol{s}}(k) &= \boldsymbol{C}_s^0\hat{\boldsymbol{x}}_s(k) + \boldsymbol{D}_s^0\boldsymbol{u}(k)\\ \boldsymbol{e}_s(k) &= \boldsymbol{s}^0(k) - \hat{\boldsymbol{s}}(k)\end{aligned} \tag{20}$$

Where $\hat{\boldsymbol{x}}_s(k) \in \mathbb{R}^{n_s}$; $\hat{\boldsymbol{s}}(k) \in \mathbb{R}^{n_s}$; the residual $\boldsymbol{e}_s(k) = \begin{bmatrix} e_{s1}(k) & e_{s2}(k) & e_{s3}(k) & \dots & e_{sq}(k)\end{bmatrix}^T \in \mathbb{R}^q$ is the residual; and $\boldsymbol{K}_s \in \mathbb{R}^{n_s x q}$ is the Kalman gain.

Status monitoring: The residuals $\boldsymbol{e}(k)$ and $\boldsymbol{e}_s(k)$ of the Kalman filters (7) and (20) are employed to monitor the status of the overall system and to detect and isolate faults in the signal and disturbance models and the sensors. The proposed scheme provides a sound framework for developing fault-tolerant systems and condition-based maintenance systems as well.

4. Evaluation on the illustrative example

The proposed two-stage identification scheme and the key properties of the Kalman filter established in the lemmas in Sections 2.3.1–2.3.3 are verified using the illustrative example given in Section 3.1. The results of this illustration are shown below in **Figure 3a** and **b**.

Subfigures A and B, of **Figure 3a** compare the true step response of the signal and its Kalman filter estimate; subfigures C and D show the output error $\boldsymbol{\vartheta}(k)$ and its estimate.

Remarks: These subfigures confirm the accuracy of the estimates of the signal and the output error (18) established in Lemmas 1 and 2. Subfigures A and B, of **Figure 3b** show the autocorrelation of the equation error whereas subfigures C and D show the autocorrelations of the residual.

Moreover, these subfigures clearly confirm that the equation error is a colored noise that is whitened by the KF, thus confirming (17) of Lemma 1 and making the KF residual a zero-man white noise process.

Table 1 compares the true and estimated poles of the signal and disturbances models. The estimated poles are obtained from the model reduction techniques employed in the second stage of the two-stage identification scheme.

Remarks: The estimated poles are close to the true ones, especially those of the signal.

5. Evaluation of the proposed scheme

The management of leakage faults in fluid systems is becoming increasingly important in recent years from the point of view of economy, potential hazards, pollution, and conservation of scarce resources. Leakage in pipes and storage tanks occurs due to faulty joints, aging, excessive loads, holes caused by corrosion and accidents and the like. The process control system is a MIMO system that exhibits

DOI: http://dx.doi.org/10.5772/intechopen.81793

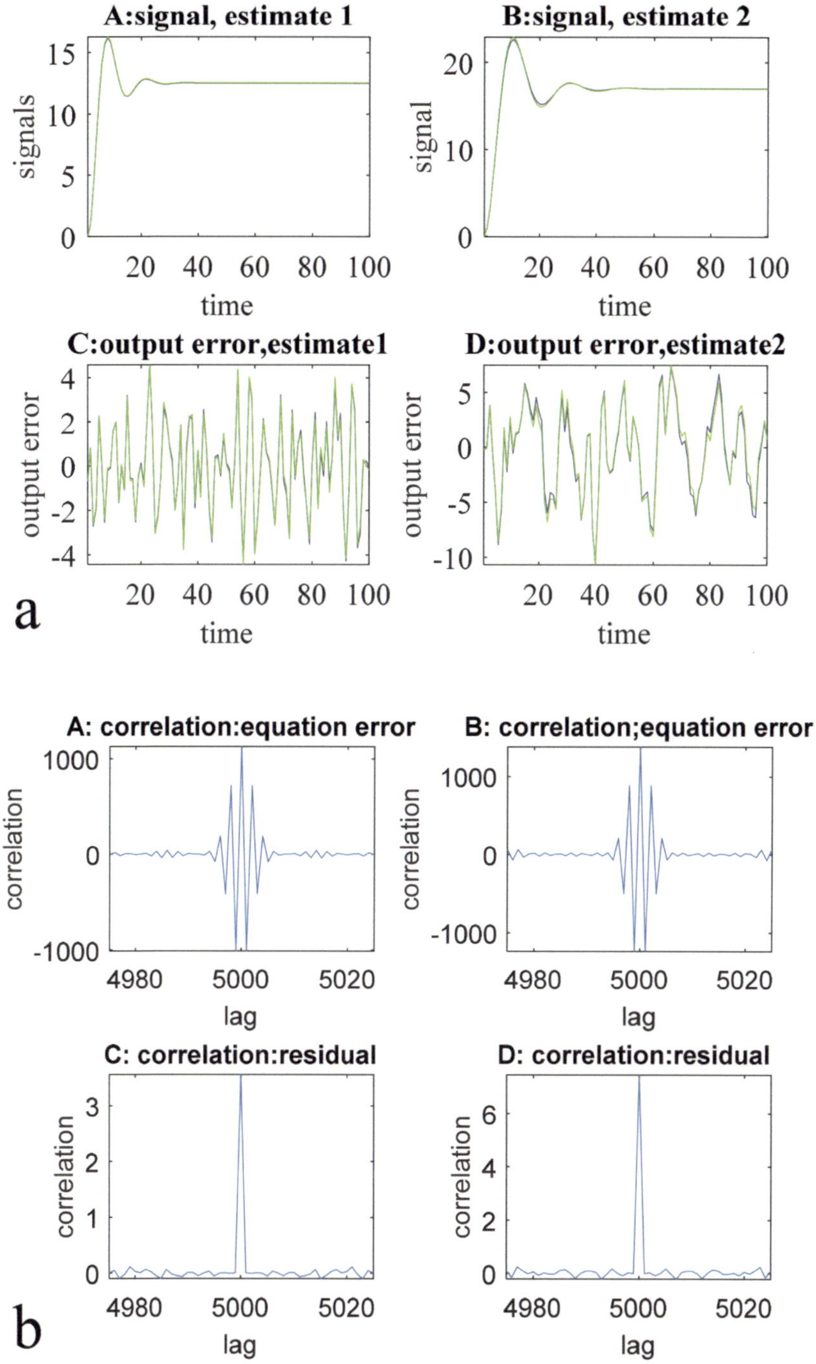

Figure 3.
(a) Signal and its estimate; output error and (b) autocorrelations of equation error and the residual and its estimate.

turbulence and is modeled as a combination of a signal, (which includes an ideal noise-free height, flow rate, and control input), a disturbance that includes effects of turbulence, and a measurement noise. The augmented model of the signal, and the disturbance, whose output is a sum of the signal, the disturbance, and the measurement noise described by Box-Jenkins model. The transfer matrices of the

	True poles	Identified poles
Signal $\hat{G}_s(z)$	$0.7500 \pm j0.3708$ $0.8500 \pm j0.2784$	$0.7510 \pm j0.3715$ $0.8483 \pm j0.2769$
Disturbance $\hat{G}_w(z)$	$0.1980 \pm j0.8737$ $0.5663 \pm j0.4114$	$0.2031 \pm j0.8752$ $0.5822 \pm j0.3746$

Table 1.
Poles of the signal and disturbance models.

signal and the disturbance may be totally different from those of the ARMA model, where the signal and the disturbance have identical denominator polynomials.

Physical systems are subject to model uncertainties and are affected to unknown stochastic disturbances such as turbulence and measurement noise. The proposed scheme covers a wider class of systems compared to the laminar flow model proposed. The laminar flow is the flow of a fluid when each particle of the fluid follows a smooth path which results in the velocity of the fluid being constant. The turbulent flow is an irregular flow that exhibits tiny whirlpool regions.

It is assumed that the disturbance is a Gaussian stochastic process and the measurement noise is a zero-mean Gaussian white noise process. The measurement output is, in general, an additive combination of the signal, disturbance and measurement noise. The output error, which is a sum of the disturbance and measurement noise, is assumed to be bounded. The signal and the disturbance are both modeled as outputs of linear time-invariant systems driven by some known input, and a Gaussian zero-mean white noise process, respectively. It is assumed that the signal, disturbance and measurement noise are mutually uncorrelated with each other.

5.1 Physical two-tank fluid system

A benchmark model is a cascade connection of a dc motor and a pump relating the reference input $r(t)$ and the flow rate $f(t)$, the outflow $q_0(t)$ and leakage $q_\ell(t)$ is a fourth-order system. The linearized signal model of the nonlinear SIMO system is:

$$\begin{bmatrix} \dot{h} \\ \dot{h}_2 \\ \dot{u} \\ \dot{f} \end{bmatrix} = \begin{bmatrix} -a_1 - \alpha & a_1 & 0 & b_1 \\ a_2 & -a_2 - \beta & 0 & 0 \\ -1 & 0 & 0 & 0 \\ -b_m k_p & 0 & b_m k_I & -a_m \end{bmatrix} \begin{bmatrix} h \\ h_1 \\ u \\ f \end{bmatrix} + \begin{bmatrix} 0 \\ 0 \\ 1 \\ b_m k_p \end{bmatrix} r(t) \tag{21}$$

Where h, h_2, u and f are respectively the height of tank 1, the height of tank 2, the control input and the flow rate; a_1, a_2, α and β are parameters associated with the linearization process, α is the leakage flow rate, $q_\ell = \alpha h$, and β is the output flow rate, $q_o = \beta h_2$. The output is given by:

$$\begin{aligned} s(k) &= [h(k) f(k)\ u(k)]^T \\ y(k) &= s(k) + d(k) + v(k) \end{aligned} \tag{22}$$

5.2 Simulation of faults in the system

The process control system is interfaced to National Instruments LABVIEW as shown below in **Figure 4a**. The controller is implemented in LABVIEW.

The two-tank system formed of subsystems and whose faults are to be isolated is shown in **Figure 4b**. There are four subsystems whose faults are to be isolated. Subsystem 1 is the flow rate sensor γ_{s1}, subsystem 2 the height sensor γ_{s2}, subsystem

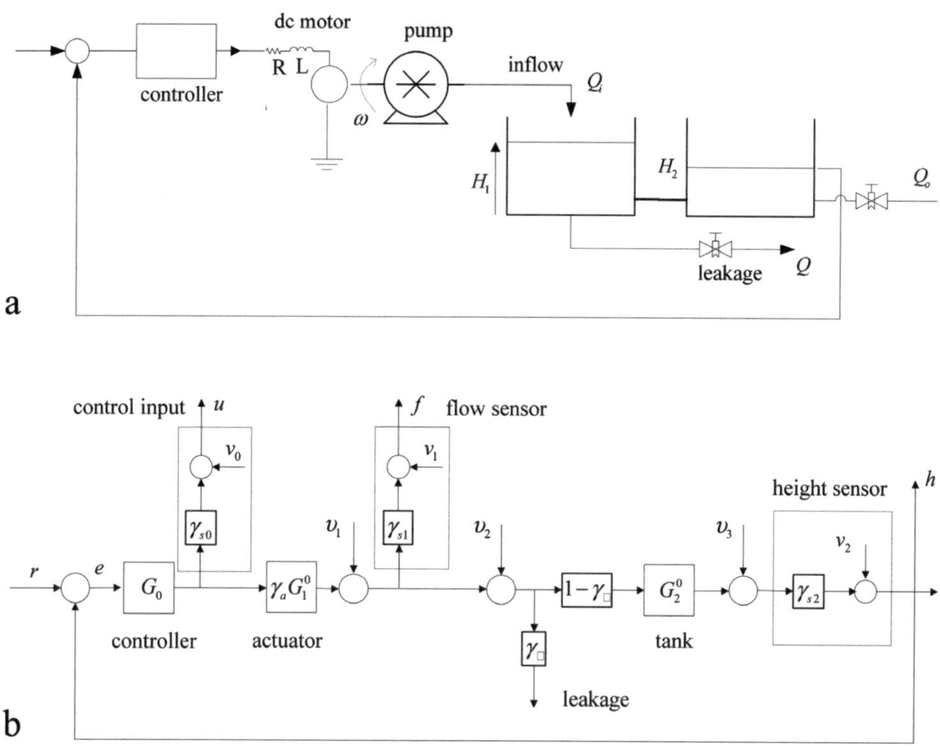

Figure 4.
(a) Two-tank fluid system controlled by LABVIEW interfaced to a PC and (b) block diagram of process control system.

3 the actuator $G_1 = G_1^0\gamma_a$ where G_1^0 is the fault-free transfer function, and subsystem 4 the leakage fault sensor gain γ_ℓ. The fault-free cases correspond to$\gamma_{si} = 1\ i = 0, 1, 2$, $\gamma_a = 1$ and $\gamma_\ell = 1$. The various subsystems and sensor blocks are all shown in **Figure 4b**. The first two blocks G_0 and $G_1 = G_1^0\gamma_a$, represent the controller and the actuator sub-systems, respectively. The leakage is modeled by the gain γ_ℓ which is used to quantify the amount of flow lost from the first tank. Thus, the net outflow from tank 1 is quantified by the gain $(1 - \gamma_\ell)$. Since the two blocks G_2^0 and $(1 - \gamma_\ell)$ cannot be dissociated from each other, they are fused into a single block labeled $G_2 = G_2^0(1 - \gamma_\ell)$. The physical two-tank system is controlled using LABVIEW which acquires the flow rate, and the height sensor outputs. The controller is implemented in LABVIEW and the controller output drives the actuator, namely the DC motor and pump combination. A fault in the sensor is introduced by including the emulator block, $\gamma_{si} : i = 0, 1, 2$ in the control input, flow rate, the height sensors, respectively in LABVIEW software. Similarly, an actuator fault is introduced by including an emulator γ_a between the controller output and the input to the DC motor. The leakage fault is simulated by opening the drainage valve of the first tank. The amount by which the valve is opened is modeled by the emulator γ_ℓ.

The height, flow rate, and control input profiles under various types of faults, are shown in **Figure 5**. Subfigures A, B and C show profiles for the leakage; subfigures D, E and F show the profiles for the actuator fault; subfigures G, H, and I show the profiles for sensor fault. The fault was simulated by varying the appropriate emulator parameters γ_ℓ, γ_a and γ_{s2}, by 0.25, 0.5 and 0.75 times their nominal values representing 'small', 'medium' and 'large' fault sizes respectively.

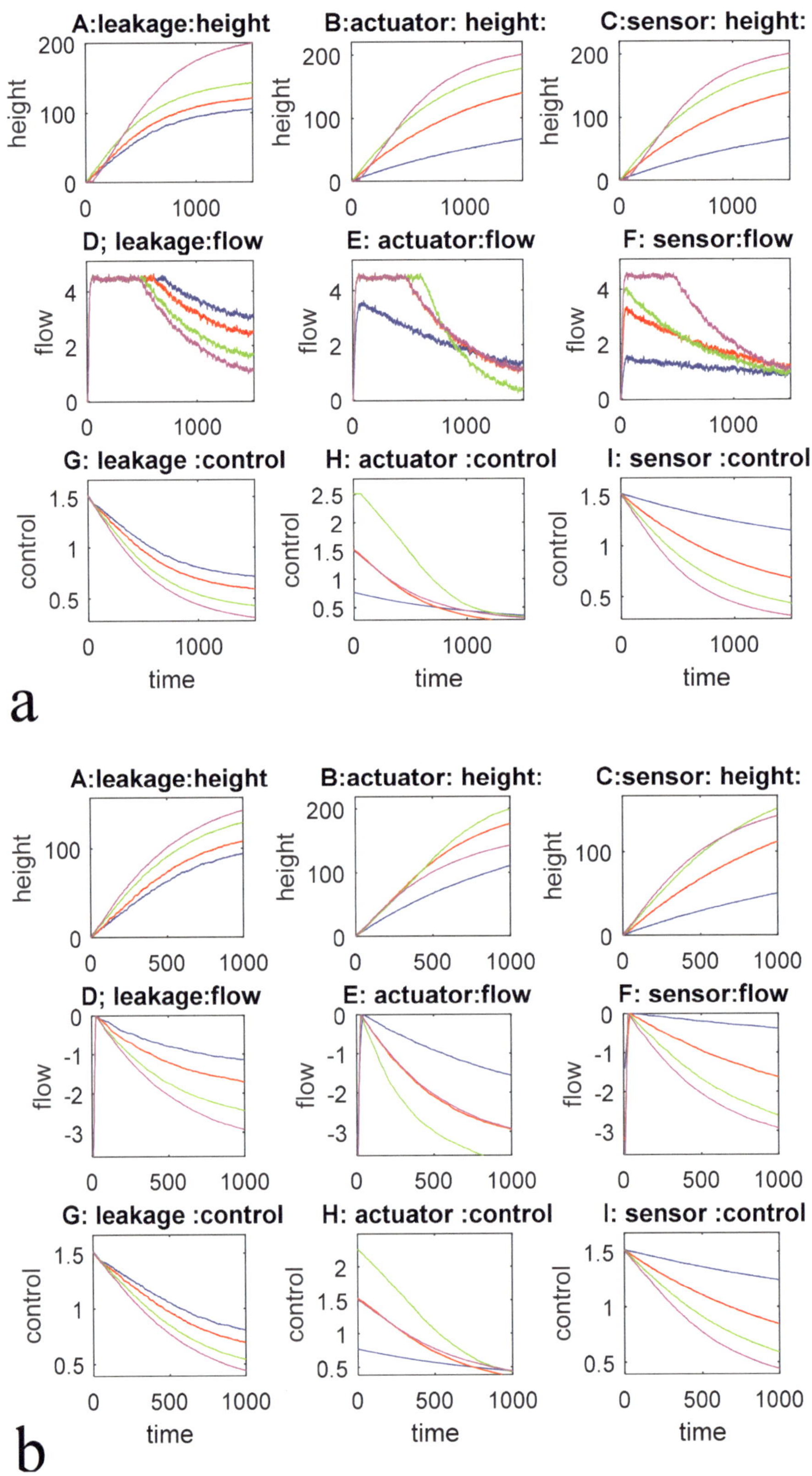

Figure 5.
(a) Height, flow rate, control: nonlinear and (b) height, flow rate, control: linearized.

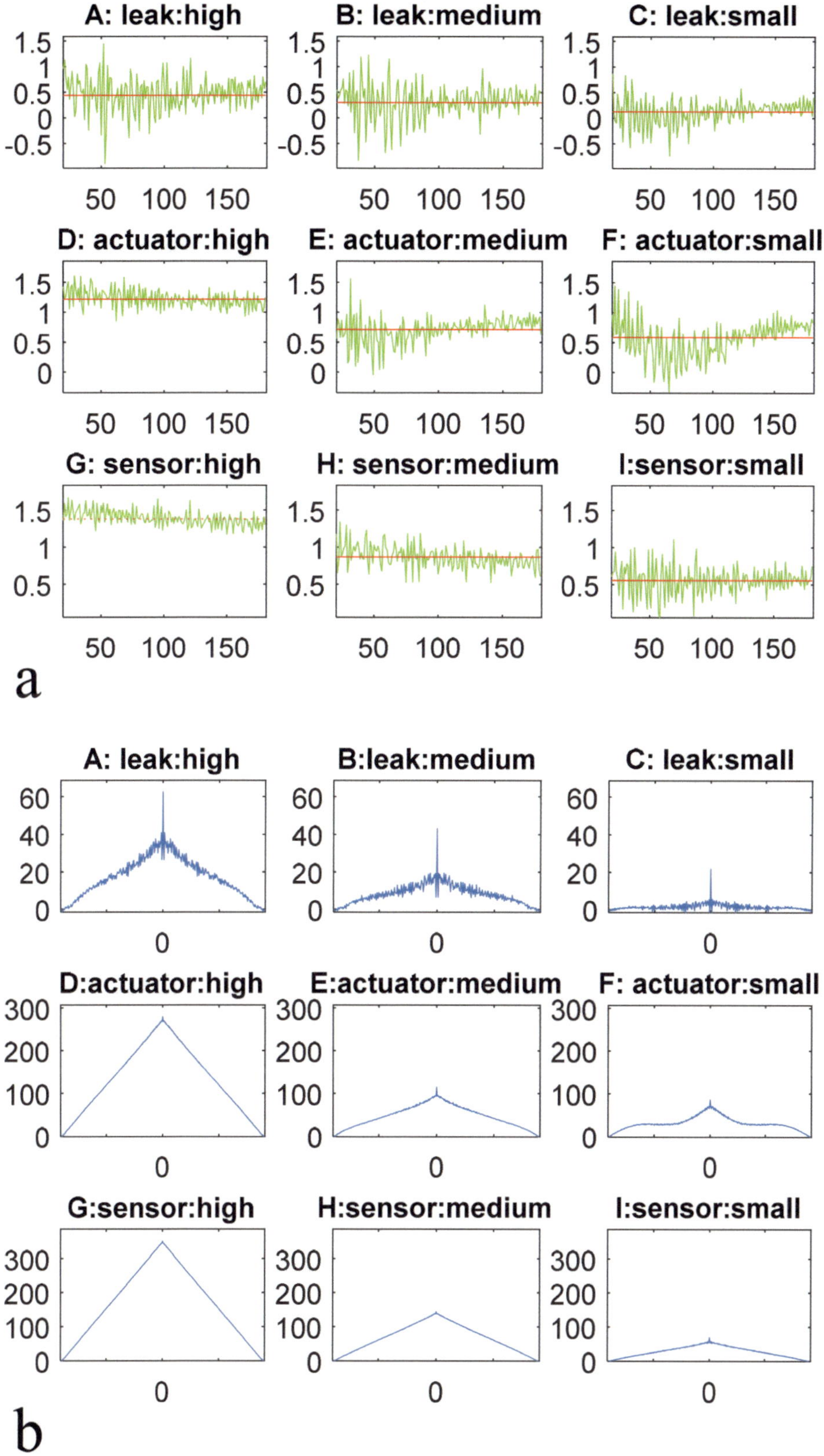

Figure 6.
(a) The residuals and test statistics and (b) autocorrelations of the residuals.

The height, the flow rate and the control input profiles under various types of faults are shown in **Figure 5a** for the nonlinear model, namely the dead-band effect of the actuator on the flow measurements. The measurement outputs are corrupted by the disturbance and measurement noise. **Figure 5b** show the outputs of the two-stage identification of the linearized signal model. Subfigures A, B and C on the top show height profiles, and subfigures D, E and F in the middle show the flow rate profiles, and G, H, and I at the bottom show the control input profiles under leakage, actuator and sensor faults, respectively. The faults are induced by varying the appropriate emulator parameters to 0.25, 0.5 and 0.75 times the nominal values to represent 'small', 'medium' and 'large' faults. However, by its control design objective, the closed-loop PI controller will hide any fault that may occur in the system and hence will make it difficult to detect it. Also, the physical system exhibits a highly-nonlinear behavior. The flow rate saturates at 4.5 ml/s. The dead-band effect in the actuator exhibits itself as a delay in the output response and saturation of the flow.

Remarks: The two-stage identification is employed to estimate the height, flow rate and the control input; their estimates are shown in **Figure 5b**. Comparing subfigures D, E, F confirms the superior performance of the identified estimates, thanks to the use of emulators.

Figure 6a shows the residuals and their test statistics, and **Figure 6b** shows the autocorrelations of the residuals when the system is subject to leakage, actuator, and sensor faults of various degrees such a small, medium and large fault sizes. Subfigures A, B, and C; D, E, and F; and G, H, and I of **Figure 6a** show the residuals and their statistics when there is a leakage, actuator and sensor faults, respectively. Subfigures A, B, and C; D, E, and F; and G, H, and I of **Figure 6b** show the corresponding auto-correlations for different fault types.

Remarks: The Bayes decision strategy was employed to assert the fault type, i.e., to decide whether it is either a leakage or an actuator or sensor fault, respectively, using the fault isolation scheme proposed in [8]. The variance of the residual, which is the maximum value of the autocorrelation function evaluated at the origin (i.e. at zero delay), indicates the fault size.

The proposed Kalman-filter-based scheme can detect and isolate small and nascent faults and estimate the fault size. Thanks to the emulator-generated data, it can also provide an accurate prognosis of the status of the system.

6. Conclusions

Emulator-based identification of a wider class of multiple-input and multiple-output system governed by Box-Jenkins model and the associated Kalman filter directly from the input-output data without a-priori knowledge of the disturbance and measurement noise statistics, and the establishment of key properties of e-stimation of the signal, the output error and their models are developed. The applications include monitoring the status of the system including faults, distinguishing between the variations in the disturbance model and those in the signal model to help diagnose a fault in the system and ensure a low false alarm probability, developing a framework for controlling autonomous vehicles, and meeting the ever-increasing need for fault-tolerant systems. The proposed emulator-based two-stage identification and estimation of the signal and its model were evaluated physical laboratory-scale process control system so as to estimate the signal corrupted by disturbance such as turbulence. Thanks to emulator-based identification, the estimates of the signal were accurate, the detection and isolation of leakage faults were promising and, as such, provide sufficient encouragement and impetus to try the proposed scheme on real-life processes in our future work.

Acknowledgements

The first author acknowledges the support of the Department of Electrical and Computer Engineering, The University of New Brunswick, and both authors acknowledge the help and suggestions of Dr. Haris Khalid.

Author details

Rajamani Doraiswami[1] and Lahouari Cheded[2]*

1 Department of Electrical and Computer Engineering, University of New Brunswick, Fredericton, New Brunswick, Canada

2 Retired Professor and Independent Higher Education Scholar and Consultant, UK

*Address all correspondence to: cheded@kfupm.edu.sa

References

[1] Ljung L. System Identification: Theory for the User. New Jersey: Prentice-Hall; 1999

[2] Doraiswami R, Cheded L. Robust Kalman filter-based least squares identification of a multi variable system. In: IET Control Theory and Applications. The Institution of Engineering and Technology; 2018. pp. 1-11. ISSN 1751-8644, www.ietdl.org

[3] Doraiswami R, Diduch C, Stevenson M. Identification of Physical Systems: Applications to Condition Monitoring, Fault Diagnosis, Soft Sensor and Controller Design. United Kingdom: John Wiley and Sons; 2014. ISBN 9781119990123

[4] Doraiswami R, Cheded L. Kalman filter for fault detection: An internal model approach. IET Control Theory and Applications. 2012;**6**(5):1-11

[5] Mendel J. Lessons in Estimation Theory in Signal Processing, Communications and Control. Englewood Cliffs, New Jersey: Prentice-Hall; 1995. ISBN0-13120981-7

[6] Doraiswami R, Cheded L. A unified approach to detection and isolation of parametric faults using a Kalman filter residuals. Journal of Franklin Institute. 2013;**350**(5):938-965

[7] Doraiswami R, Cheded L. Linear parameter varying modelling and identification for condition-based monitoring of systems. Journal of Franklin Institute. 2015;**352**(4): 1766-1790

[8] Doraiswami R, Cheded L. Robust fault tolerant control using an accurate emulator-based identification technique. International Journal of Control. 2017. ISSN: 0020-7179 (Print) 1366-5820 (Online). Available from: http://www.tandfonline.com/loi/tcon20. http://dx.doi.org/10.1080/00207179.2017.1318452

[9] Di Ruscio D. Closed and open loop subspace identification of the Kalman filter. Modelling Identification and Control. 2009;**30**(2):71-86. ISSN: 1890-1328

[10] Qin JS. Overview of subspace identification. Computer and Chemical Engineering. 2006;**30**:1502-1513

[11] Jansson M. A New Subspace Method for Open and Closed Loop Data. Prague, Czech Republic: IFAC World Congress; 2005

[12] Kumaresan R, Tufts DW. Estimating exponentially damped sinusoids and pole-zero mapping. IEEE Transactions on Acoustics, Speech and Signal Processimng. December 1982; **30**(6):833

[13] Porat B, Friedlander B. On the accuracy of the Kumaresan-tufts method for estimating complex damped exponentials. IEEE Transactions on Acoustics, Speech, and Signal Processing. 1987:**35**(2):231-235

[14] Forssell U, Ljung L. Closed loop identification revisited. Automatica. 1999;**35**(7):1215-1241

[15] Mallory GWJ, Doraiswami R. A frequency domain identification scheme for control and fault diagnosis. ASME Transactions on Dynamics, Measurement, and Control. 1997;**119**: 48-56

[16] Doraiswami R. A two-stage identification with application to control, feature extraction, and spectral estimation. IEE Proceedings: Control Theory and Applications. 2005;**152**(4): 379-386

[17] Doraiswami R, Cheded L. High-order least squares identification: A new approach. In: Proceedings of the International Conference of Control, Dynamic Systems and Robotics. Ottawa, ON, Canada; 2014

[18] Gugercin S, Antoulas A. A survey of model reduction by balanced truncation some new results. International Journal of Control. 2004;**47**(8):748-766

[19] Han J, Zhang H, Wang Y, Liu Y. Disturbance observer-based fault estimation and dynamic output feedback with local nonlinear models. ISA Transactions. 2015;**59**:114-124